War! Hellish War!
Star Shell Reflections
1916–1918

War! Hellish War!
Star Shell Reflections
1916–1918

The Illustrated Great War Diaries of
Jim Maultsaid

Barbara McClune

Pen & Sword
MILITARY

First published in Great Britain in 2016 by
Pen & Sword Military
an imprint of
Pen & Sword Books Ltd
47 Church Street
Barnsley
South Yorkshire S70 2AS

ISBN 978 1 47387 943 0

Typeset in Ehrhardt by
Mac Style Ltd, Bridlington, East Yorkshire
Printed and bound by Replika Press Pvt. Ltd.

Pen & Sword Books Ltd incorporates the imprints of Pen & Sword
Archaeology, Atlas, Aviation, Battleground, Discovery, Family History,
History, Maritime, Military, Naval, Politics, Railways, Select, Social
History, Transport, True Crime, and Claymore Press, Frontline Books,
Leo Cooper, Praetorian Press, Remember When, Seaforth Publishing
and Wharncliffe.

For a complete list of Pen & Sword titles please contact
PEN & SWORD BOOKS LIMITED
47 Church Street, Barnsley, South Yorkshire, S70 2AS, England
E-mail: enquiries@pen-and-sword.co.uk
Website: www.pen-and-sword.co.uk

PART TWO

of

STAR SHELL

REFLECTIONS

BY

JIM MAULTSAID

THE SOMME 1915-16

JULY 1ST

BIG BATTLE

WOUNDED HOSPITAL DAYS

THE DEPÔT

CAMBRIDGE

A NEW LIFE IN THE C.L.C

Foreword

I put before you *War! Hellish War!* the latest volume of *Star Shell Reflections* as written and illustrated by my Grandfather, Jim Maultsaid. When reading this book you will witness the typical spirit of the 14th Royal Irish Rifles (YCV) embodied throughout Jim's stories and sketches.

The original works are in four large, bound journals, written all in ink and brilliantly illustrated with everything taken from the little pocket books he carried in the trenches.

In this volume, Jim begins his time with the Chinese Labour Corps, a little known entity of the Great War.

I am honoured to have these unique works published and, in doing so, sincerely believe that the selfless contribution of Jim Maultsaid and all those brave young men who fought with him will live on in history and may inspire future generations.

This book is dedicated to their memory.

Barbara Anne McClune

Introduction

This book is not intended as a History of the Great War. It is just a record of events that appealed to me.

As a young lad when I joined the 14th Royal Irish Rifles (YCV) in 1914 I began to keep a record of my experiences and, over the years, my journal grew until it filled several large volumes with my writings and sketches.

All young eager soldiers, we were thrown together by the whirlpool of war and we took the path which led to the slopes of Thiepval and the Battle of the Somme.

Our life day by day is all here. Our sorrows, our trials and troubles and tears and sadness, but I have also tried my best to give you a glimpse of the bright side and an insight into the lives of those wonderful pals of mine.

Reader, I must tell you once again these are my experience and that of my chums as it is impossible to tell what is happening outside the range of my sight on this terrible battle for the ridge.

Wounded, I returned to England and yet, in 1918, I find myself back in the war commissioned into the Chinese Labour Corps.

Did I ever in my wildest dreams imagine for a moment that I would spend a good part of my army career as a lieutenant in the Chinese Labour Corps? I did not … but I was a welcome volunteer that cold winter's morning in Boulogne.

Jim Maultsaid

"AFTER THE STORM"

THE RE-ACTION SETS IN. WE GET THE NEWS——

THE dawn breaks. First a slight uplifting of the darkness, a faint glimmer of the sky, and the dawn of another day.

DEATH AND DESTRUCTION

All night long we had been on duty, every mother's son of us – hours of horror – and destruction. Death had stalked among us. We had walked in 'Death's Valley'. Young boys had faced the reaper and faced him with a stout heart. Dirty, unwashed pallid faces, strained and staring eyes looked out from beneath the tin hats. Old faces now! Old in experience. At the point of complete collapse – but duty first. 'Here come the tea churns Sergeant!' I start up. The boys gather round, fill up their Dixie tins, and drink.

The lookout sentry shouts 'Come here Sergeant. What's this?' I jump up on the firestep and gaze out across the shell-torn ground, over to the German trenches. 'My God! They're coming!' But wait! A dirty white cloth of some kind bobs up and down! A signal. 'Hold on boys. Don't fire yet.' A figure appears. Then out comes another. Several more follow. Germans? Sure enough! But they are carrying something. What's the game? Should we fire? 'No! No! It's a Red Cross squad – out to pick up wounded – leave them alone', and we did. We watched – all alert. Slowly the rescue party gathered their burdens together, and carried them back – back through their wire and into their trenches – whilst we watched this strange scene. Not a shot did we fire! War is war! But we were only human.

So we had stopped a raiding party? Or was it an attack?

AFTER THE STORM.

DEATH AND DESTRUCTION.

WHY SO STILL?

WE WATCH A STRANGE SCENE — SHOULD WE FIRE?

GLAD YOU ARE SAFE ERNIE.

NO MORE MARCHING!
NO MORE SONGS WITH US!
NEVER MORE TO SHARE "OUR BILLET"

SKETCHES BY JIM MAULTSAID FROM MY WAR SKETCH BOOK 1916

HERE SAVAGE TAKE A SHOVEL

DOWN.... DOWN..... DOWN....
I GRAB A HANDFUL OF BARBED WIRE.

WE GUARD THE WIRING PARTY – MY BOMBING SQUAD.

MUFFLED THUDS!
WILL JERRY HEAR US?

ALL THE WORLD FLOATS AWAY....

GERMAN WIRE.

SKETCHED BY ME IN 1916. JUST BEFORE THE NIGHT OF HORROR

OUT TO THE WORLD.

BEAUMONT HAMEL FROM THE BRITISH LINES.

BAD NEWS

During the early hours we find touch with 29th Division. And the news that came through was – well, it was bad. Jerry had been over on a raiding expedition with about one hundred men or so, and carried back some scores of these 29th boys as prisoners of war. He had blown in dug-outs. He killed dozens. He had, in fact, wrecked their trenches – and wrecked them!

We assisted as best we could to restore order again. It was a shambles! We extended our front to the left and took over some more duties.

... AND THE 14TH?

And the 14th lads? Yes, we suffered too! Some two score or so would never, never march with us again, would never sing with us, would never play – and would never more share our 'billets'. Ah! It was awful to stand and get the word, 'He's gone Sergeant!' 'Yes! Killed! … Killed! … Killed!'

STOP MOPING AROUND

'Stop moping around Savage! Take a shovel here, and join this fatigue squad for trench repair work.' 'Here McClay, lend a hand to take this back – back!'

Why did my brain burn? Throbbing like a steam-hammer. The blood rushed to my head – then down the back of my spine! Steady yourself Jim! Hell! My head was reeling!

Slipping down … down in the chalk … I grabbed a handful of barbed wire … fell amongst it … and was all cut and torn. A mighty effort and I worked out my water bottle – to have a drink of cold tea. I was revived again. Thank the Lord not one of my men had witnessed this weakness of the flesh!

WHY SO STILL

Tom Murphy passed – Sergeant Tom! Directing his squad of stretcher-bearers. Why were some covered with blankets? And so still! I crush back against the trench. I salute! They pass on … on … their last journey!

GLAD YOU ARE SAFE

Sections were re-formed. New faces filled up gaps. No. 2 Platoon was remodelled. Sergeant Major Ernest Powell was busy with pencil and notebook. 'Glad you are safe Ernie,' I whispered! We shook hands – that old pal and I. 'What about Sergeant Billy Kelly?' 'Yes! Billy is safe and well.' 'Fine! Fine! What about A Company?' 'Didn't hear.' And B? 'Pretty bad!' 'And C?' ' Lost some good boys!' 'D Company?' 'Poor old D, we had a big list! Captain Willis is breaking his heart about "his boys".'

REPAIRS

MUFFLED thuds, we drive the wooden stakes. Raw hands, sore bleeding hands. Pass the cruel barbs through – and around in loops. We are out now wiring, in the dead of night – a summer's night.

I have my bombing section out as a covering party, to see that our wire repairers are not taken by surprise. We lie in the long grass quite flat: all wide awake, some are occupying the rim of a large shell hole. Ears to the ground, we guard the troops. Thud! Thud! Thud! Flash! A bunch of coloured lights soar away up from behind the German trenches, arch over above us, and burst like a rainbow in the sky. Were we discovered?

All is quiet! Again the dull sound, coming to us through the earth as our big wooden mallets strike the stakes. Surely Jerry can hear that?

Zip! Zip! Rat-a-tat! Rat – a – tat! Down closer to mother earth go our heads as that ugly sound crashes out. Jerry's guns! Bang! Bang! Whack! Showers of sparks. Ping! A bullet strikes metal of some kind and soars away. Quietness. We again breathe freely.

Zirr – ip! Zirr-ip! Like a blue flash they passed over our heads. Two shells plunging through the night air – to crash with a mighty roar somewhere in our reserve lines. Which company is in reserve? Why should this question trouble me? I don't know! But it did.

Zip! Zip! Up goes some clay. Quite close to my left hand. 'Are you alright Rogers?' I whisper? 'Yes! Quite right, Sergeant.'

THE STRAIN IS TELLING

I'm wet. What has made it all wet around me? It's raining, softly, and has been for some time. In the excitement of the moment we had not noticed. We are now almost wet through. How long have we been out? I can't say! My eyes are heavy. No sleep for several days and nights. The strain is telling. Whack – bang! I start up. Down on the right flank it bursts – and the showers of clay chalk falls over us. Heavens! But that one was near. Is it starting tonight – all over again? Surely to God not.

No sound from the wiring party. 'Crawl back Rooney and see if they are finished,' I pass back the command.

COME IN BOYS

Something dark in front of me. 'Hist!' What is it I wondered? My gun, a big six-shooter goes up to the alert. I strain my eyes. Moving? Yes! I half rose to meet the enemy. Another movement – and I'll fire. The figure crouched down – and speaks. 'Is that you Sergeant Maultsaid?' 'Yes!' I whisper. 'Lieutenant Monard says you are to bring your men in now.' Thank God! 'Come on boys, back we go – but don't be rash.'

WE COULD HAVE HUGGED HIM

Crawling back, yard by yard, we gain our wire – and crawl through, to slide down, all safe! How secure we felt once more.

Lieutenant Monard awaits us. 'Go and have a sleep, boys.' We could have hugged him. Dead tired, deadbeat, we totter to the little dug-outs, and fling our bodies down. All the world floats away. Asleep before the body touches the floor. It would have taken a dozen batteries outside the shelter to have awakened us.

FROM MY RECORDS

Early that morning the fatigue squads were busy on this stretch of pasture land that had been selected as our sports field for the day's events.

Our captain and Adjutant, Captain Mulholland, was a great believer in sport items for the troops – and I agreed with his views.

THE YCV BAND DOES ITS STUFF

Dinner over, we made a bee-line for the sports ground. Our battalion band was giving us some fine tunes and all the 14th were there to a man. The fun commenced. Regimental Sergeant Major Elphic was master of ceremonies. He bawled out his orders and the first event was underway.

HEATS ARE RUN OFF

Competition was keen – each company had its selected stalwarts – and opening heats were run off, to sort the wheat from the chaff.

D COMPANY YELLS ITS APPROVAL

Groans! Cheers! Excitement! The fun was fast – and furious. Now for the big event of the day. Line up for first heat of one hundred yards. Flash! Off they go – but I'm only a spectator. One, two, three – home they come! Heats two and three, and several more, are run off. The entry is a big one. My heat comes round.

I won easily – D Company yells its approval.

I FAIL DISMALLY

Bomb throwing! It fell to my famous thrower 'Ned' Kelly. He was a whopper. The mile race went to B Company and was deserved.

All the fun of the fair in the obstacle race – under tarpaulins to emerge as black as your boots. Through a barrel that kept bobbing about. Over a couple of limber wagons, then

BATTALION SPORTS PICTURES.

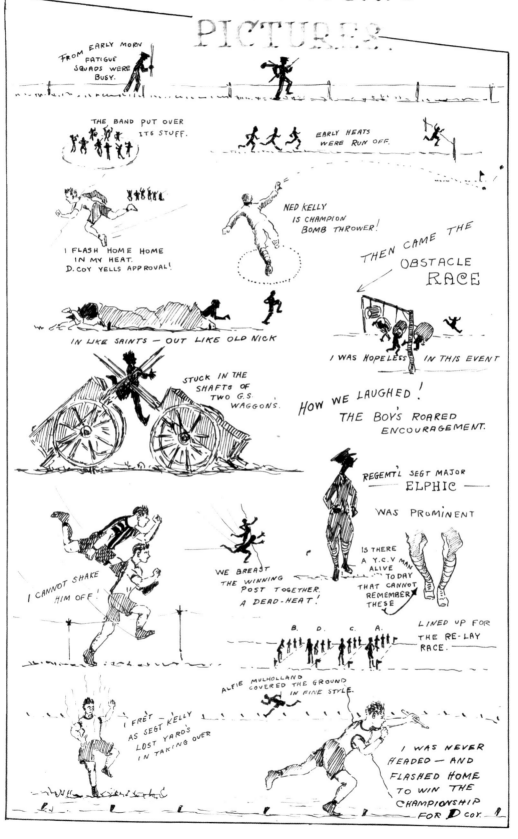

FROM EARLY MORN FATIGUE SQUADS WERE BUSY.

THE BAND PUT OVER ITS STUFF.

EARLY HEATS WERE RUN OFF.

I FLASH HOME HOME IN MY HEAT. D. COY YELLS APPROVAL!

NED KELLY IS CHAMPION BOMB THROWER!

THEN CAME THE OBSTACLE RACE

IN LIKE SAINTS — OUT LIKE OLD NICK

I WAS HOPELESS IN THIS EVENT

STUCK IN THE SHAFTS OF TWO G.S. WAGGONS.

HOW WE LAUGHED! THE BOY'S ROARED ENCOURAGEMENT.

REGEMT'L SEGT MAJOR ELPHIC WAS PROMINENT

IS THERE A Y.C.V MAN ALIVE TO DAY THAT CANNOT REMEMBER THESE

I CANNOT SHAKE HIM OFF!

WE BREAST THE WINNING POST TOGETHER. A DEAD-HEAT!

B. D. C. A.

LINED UP FOR THE RE-LAY RACE.

ALFIE MULHOLLAND COVERED THE GROUND IN FINE STYLE.

I FRET KELLY AS SEGT KELLY LOST YARDS IN TAKING OVER

I WAS NEVER HEADED — AND FLASHED HOME TO WIN THE CHAMPIONSHIP FOR D COY.

down the straight for 'home'. I was hopelessly stuck in a barrel – and came in when the 'night was falling'. Lost! Not my line, this game! Come on A Company! And they did!

THE BIG RACE – DEAD HEAT FIRST PLACE

Line up for final of the hundred yards dash. Tense excitement! The starting pistol flashed – and 'off' like greyhounds. How I ran! I'm winning! I can hear the full-throated cries of the watching crowds. All is clear each side of me. I'm now for the final plunge – and the tape!

A big figure looms up beside me – from the rear. Can I hold out – to win?

Come on! Come on – Jim! The figure on my right is holding its place. I cannot shake him off. Home! A dead heat. First Sergeant Maultsaid, First Lance Corporal Crothers. We shake hands. A great race, chum.

THE OLD FIRM FLASH HOME IN RELAY RACE

Fall in for the relay race. Four runners from each company, and the Battalion championship at stake. We draw for position. Our famous D lot were strong in this department, and we had hopes of 'lifting' the race. I was No.4 runner – and the distance was a two hundred yards dash, the last lap of the race. How I fretted as Sergeant Kelly lost yards in the taking over from No.1, but he made it up – to pass the baton over to No.3 almost alongside his nearest rival. Good old D. Alfie Mulholland covered the ground in fine style to hand me the 'stick' – and away I went. I was never headed – and flashed 'home' to win for the famous D Company.

OFF DUTY WE TAKE A STROLL – AND VISIT THE FAMOUS TOWN OF CATHEDRAL FAME – AND

GET A SURPRISE!

COME ON SERGEANT – come for a stroll? Sure, but where can we go? Several of my platoon chums asked me to have a walk. The day was a free one, and we were 'resting' some little distance back behind the line. 'Let's go away down this road to the right, Sergeant, I would like to see what the country is like in these parts.' We had never been on this ground before, but we knew that the large town of Albert lay somewhere in this direction. A hot summer's day. Like schoolboys, out on a ramble, we just rambled on, and on. Kilo after kilo was covered; we rested by the roadside to wipe the sweat away.

A big steep embankment was now on our right. We crossed a little bridge. Was the river beneath the Ancre? Or the Somme? We did not know.

SKETCHES OF INTEREST.

LIKE SCHOOLBOYS WE SET OUT.

IN THE SUNLIGHT. OUR FIRST VIEW OF ALBERT.

THE ENTRANCE TO THE TRENCHES GAVE US A START.

PICTURES BY TIM MAULTSMO

I GO UPSTAIRS. ALL WAS CONFUSION.

THE MEAL-THAT WAS NEVER FINISHED.

A BIG SPOON PURE LEAD I TOOK IT AS A SOUVENIR.

DOWN ON THE COBBLE STONES. I THROW MYSELF.

A BIG BLACK HOLE APPEARS.

SHE BECKONS TO ME

I DASH ACROSS!

La Guerre 1914-15 — ALBERT (Somme) - Ce qui reste de la magnifique Église après le dernier bombardement
231. R. P., Paris — Albert (Somme) – Rimains of splendid church after the bombardment

HOW MUCH MADAM.?

ZIP'-ZIP! THE BULLETS DOWN THE STREET.

THE GERMAN TRENCHES ON THE TOP OF THE HILL.

I BEAT IT BACK TO SAFTEY!

OUT FOR FUN – LIKE SCHOOLBOYS

The entrance to the communication trench gave us a start. Were we so near the front as all that? The ground round about was shell-marked – and the trees were blackened. A sure sign of war! 'Say! Chums this place is dangerous looking.' Still forward we go, round a curve in the road – and there before us in the sunlight stood the church spire with the figure sticking out 'crossways', not upright. We gazed in wonderment! How did it hang like that? And no support! A wild desire to have a close-up view of this sight took possession of me, but was the town out of bounds to us – a bunch of boys from 36th Division who were out for some sightseeing? We circled round the outskirts, then sneaked down a back street – and were in the town.

FEAR! HOPE! DREAD!

Crash – bang! Back to real 'war' again. A big German shell smashes down into the houses somewhere in the forefront and we crouch against the wall of a house. Not a sinner did we meet – so far – either dead or alive. I am now all alone. My pals have moved on in front of me. I glance through a window, as a white tablecloth caught my eye, and can see through the dust and grime that the table is laid for lunch. Funny looking! I hesitate, then decide to enter. The window is barred on the inside. I tried the door. Locked. Putting my shoulder to it, I heaved and it gave way. The smell of decay was in the air. I made my way to the front room. There sat the table all laid out for a meal – a meal that was never finished. All was confusion and disorder. Chairs overturned, pictures smashed on the floor – and the dust almost a couple of inches thick spread over everything. Just picture that scene in the early days of 1914! The family of five (I counted the layout of the table) get the news of the Huns coming. Fear! hope! and dread take possession of them. Then fear wins and the family flee from the dreaded 'Huns'. No doubt about it – the Germans were feared and hated by the French – not without reason, I suppose. I go up the stairs. All is confusion. The marks of my feet stand out in the dust. Long enough here I think, and return to the front room once more.

In the middle of the table stands a soup urn and a big spoon sticks out. Here's a souvenir. I take the spoon. It was a black colour and pure lead. It stayed with me for a long time, but eventually I lost it – my 'memento of Albert'.

BANG! – WHIZZ! – WHIZZ!

Out into the fresh air again. What a relief! Where have my mates got to? Not a sign of life anywhere. The purr of an aeroplane overhead. I look up. A German machine far up in the blue sky. Is he spotting for guns? Bang! Whizz – Whizz. Black puffs of smoke hang over the street. I hear bricks and masonry falling. Glass splinters somewhere. I throw myself flat on the cobblestones as it roars past – a bright flash! –and a big shell crashes into the side of the shuttered house some twenty yards behind me, leaving a black ugly hole. The fumes flowed down. Dust and smoke. I choke and cough.

THE SHOCK OF MY LIFE!

Next second I get the shock of my life! A voice, in fluent French, shouts something to me. I look up and see an old Frenchwoman beckon me to come over. I rise up and dash over through the open door to find myself in? – What do you think? A little shop. Here she was, this old mother of France, right in the firing line almost, selling her souvenirs. 'Merci, madame!' I gasped. She laughed! 'No bon! Sergon,' pointing a long thin finger to the street outside. I agree!

I BUY A MEMENTO – OF ALBERT

'How much for the brooch, madame?' It was a little affair like this. 'Two Francs, Sergon.' I replied 'Bon' and passed her a five-franc note. The change was offered, and refused. She bestowed her gratitude and thanks. 'Do you stop here all by yourself mother,' I asked? I repeat the question, make signs and she understands me, she does, makes a sign of the cross – and I take it she trusts in God, and hangs on to her own home. What faith! I wonder did she come through the years – with her faith – and live?

I CLEAR OUT – TO SAFETY

I say farewell and open the front door once more. She mutters a prayer. I depart. Zip! Zip! Zup! Bullets now right down the street. The German trenches show up white – on the crest of the hills – and I run – for safety.

OFTEN in the days gone past I had looked out, and over at this wood away on our right – and watched the big black 'Jack Johnsons' bursting in it – until it looked like a black curtain against the skyline. And now the YCVs were actually to hold this line. It was our first spell in Thiepval Wood. What would it feel like to be under fire, amongst the tall and gaunt trees? And hear the shells crashing again against the blackened stump of a once proud tree! Yes! It would be also strange to us. A fine communication trench named Elgin Avenue led right in, and up to the front line almost. Deep and broad, it was easy to work forward to our battle positions.

VERY STRANGE

Halfway up this trench was one of the strangest things I ever met on my travels in the trench zone – and that was a water tap that gave us a supply of pure, fresh water, a godsend to the troops. Where it came from I know not, but many a petrol tin of that glorious stuff was carried by us to our dug-outs.

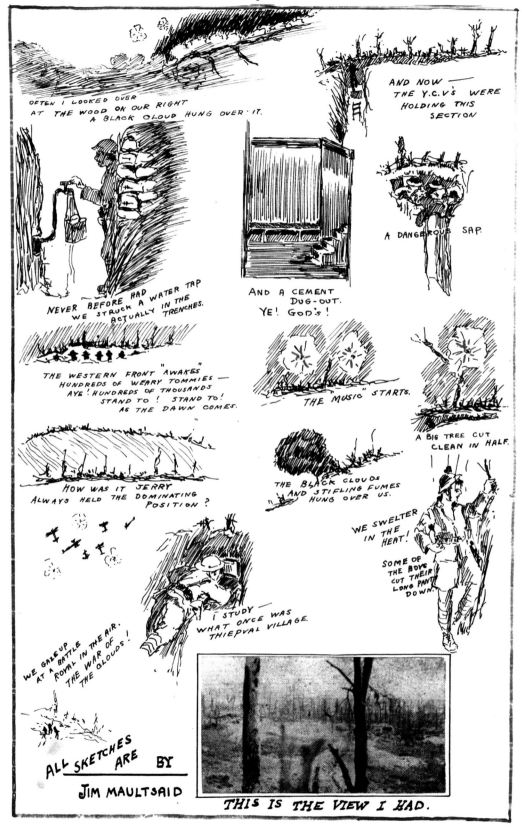

A WOOD — OF HORRORS!

OFTEN I LOOKED OVER AT THE WOOD ON OUR RIGHT A BLACK CLOUD HUNG OVER IT.

AND NOW — THE Y.C.V'S WERE HOLDING THIS SECTION

A DANGEROUS SAP.

NEVER BEFORE HAD WE STRUCK A WATER TAP ACTUALLY IN THE TRENCHES.

AND A CEMENT DUG-OUT. YE! GOD'S!

THE WESTERN FRONT "AWAKES" HUNDREDS OF WEARY TOMMIES — AYE! HUNDREDS OF THOUSANDS STAND TO! STAND TO! AS THE DAWN COMES.

THE "MUSIC" STARTS.

A BIG TREE CUT CLEAN IN HALF.

HOW WAS IT JERRY ALWAYS HELD THE DOMINATING POSITION?

THE BLACK CLOUDS AND STIFLING FUMES HUNG OVER US.

WE SWELTER IN THE HEAT!

SOME OF THE BOYS CUT THEIR LONG PANTS DOWN.

WE GAZE UP AT A BATTLE ROYAL IN THE AIR. THE WAR OF THE CLOUDS!

I STUDY — WHAT ONCE WAS THIEPVAL VILLAGE.

ALL SKETCHES ARE BY JIM MAULTSAID

THIS IS THE VIEW I HAD.

CEMENT! YE GODS!

Here in this wood I came across the first British dug-out that could boast cement sides – at least it was the first I ever came across. With iron girders for a roof! Ye Gods! But later I found it required them.

THE WESTERN FRONT WAKES UP!

During the night hours we had taken over from the Skins.[1] They said it was a great relief to get rid of this d★★★ show for a week or so. Not too bright, this kind of talk, from old, seasoned warriors! I did not feel too happy, as I allotted my section their various quarters and posted my sentries. A sap ran out into our wire – this required two men – and our instructions were: 'it's dangerous; Jerry has it taped. Keep low in the early hours of the dawn; he riddles the place with machine guns.' By heavens he did. The dawn comes slowly. Gradually the Western Front comes to life. Hundreds of weary Tommies – aye! Hundreds of thousands – French, British, and German troops line the firestep and await the coming of another day. Crash! Crack! Crack! Zip! Zip! Zip! The music has started. Leaves and branches flutter down. Shot through by bullets. A ripping – rending – splitting sound. There goes a big tree split in half by a direct shell hit – and we duck as the upper half falls smashing down, right across our front-line trench. Sure death for any unfortunate Tommy who would stand in its path.

HOW DID WE GET THEM?

The usual 'strafe' wore itself out! We banged five rounds apiece across, and at the white chalk trenches up at the top of the rising ground. As usual, we held the low-lying part of the ground; Jerry always seemed to have 'clicked' the dominating positions. It was the same here. Did he dig in first – then let us come forward and take what was left?

PLONK! SWISH – SWISH!

Plonk! Swish – swish! They fell in our sector with the regularity of clockwork. Daylight now – but rest was unthinkable. The black smoke and the fumes hung over us – like a pall! What a show!

Surely the enemy had lots of 'stuff' to throw away. Or did he not like the look of this wood? Did it hide too much? I'm sure he would have liked to know more about us – and our 'doings'.

WE SWELTER!

The sun shines down. We swelter in the heat. Collars are opened. Some of the boys have cut their long pants down – and made 'shorts', all for easy comfort. Sweat pours down!

Crack! Crack! Crack! How the bullets fly through the branches. Lots of firewood here, but we don't require fires – it's warm enough in all conscience.

A WAR OF THIER OWN

In the blue sky thousands of feet up a battle royal is in progress. We gaze up and take a deep interest in the 'war' of the clouds. Friend and foe are all one to us. We cannot make them

---

1. The nickname of the Royal Inniskilling Fusiliers was the 'Skins'.

out – but the 'antics' of the small black dots give us something to look at – and I marvel at the pluck of friend and foe away up there trying to kill each other. A war of their own! Bad enough on land – but up there!

FINDING MY BEARINGS
I take a stroll along our front-line trenches. I want to get the layout of the land more or less. I'm mixed up with another company now – on my right!

OURS – FOR A LITTLE WHILE
'Yes! Sergeant, that's Thiepval village.' A smart sentry points a thumb out to his front. I'm interested. Through a square box look-out contrivance I gaze long at a pile of white chalk and tumbled down masonry. A spot that was to cause many anxious months of anxiety and the loss of many valuable lives in the days to come. In fact this point was holding out long after our lines had closed in on it, on three sides; a regular 'thorn' in the flesh of our armies during the Battle of the Somme. Yet! we, the 36th (Ulster) Division, had it within our grasp on 1 July 1916. But lack of support lost us the golden opportunity. It was not part of our objective this day – but the Ulstermen in the wild spirit of advance swept round on it and took it from Jerry, only to be cleared out owing to the 32nd and the 29th Divisions on our flanks failing to make any headway – but I'll tell you this story later.

CAUSE TO REMEMBER
Shelled day and night for a solid week – we had cause to remember THE WOOD.

ACROSS THE SUNKEN ROAD.
A STORY OF NARROW ESCAPE FROM CAPTURE—IN NO-MANS-LAND.

'JIM! I want you to come along with me tonight – on a little "stunt" out there!' Lieutenant Wedgwood gave me this command, and request, so of course I said 'Yes, sure. What time do we "kick off" at?' 'Oh! About 12.30 tonight Sergeant.'

Mr Wedgwood was a great chum of mine – and we had often explored no man's land together. Not my platoon officer, but as we were both of the same bent, and 'Scouts' by nature, it appealed to us; the opportunity to explore was much better than standing in mud and water for weeks on end, hence our jobs beyond our wires.

Lieutenant Monard did not object, so the way was clear for our adventure. This front was new to us. We had never been out on the right of the swamp and our business tonight was a survey of the German position along this front.

Together, we spent hours planning, studying, and weighing up our route. A sunken road ran through the waste ground out beyond, and the shell holes were very numerous. Useful sometimes, in times of trouble, but were known to often contain a party of the enemy, so were worth being careful about.

YOU LOOK FUNNY!

You look funny! And I did. The little pocket looking-glass revealed a black-faced strange individual. Lieutenant Wedgwood laughed at me – I had a good laugh at him – so we both enjoyed the joke. Down in a little dug-out our faces had received a coat of black boot polish, the pockets were emptied, all badges removed – and buttons blackened. My six-shooter had been carefully oiled and cleaned, a Mills bomb in each pocket and we were all ready.

OVER AND OUT

A good night for our errand. Dark, but calm, and very warm. We passed several of our sentries on our way to the front line – the password was given – and we clambered up, out, and over the parapet – our journey commenced.

ZIP! PING! ZIP!

A passage through our wire, and we were clear of all obstacles.

An odd bullet 'sizzed' past. Some night flares were sailing up into the dark heavens away on our right flank – down towards Albert.

Steady progress forward – and we slid slowly into the sunken road. Good enough so far! About halfway now. Up the opposite bank and then down on our bellies – like snakes in the grass. What grass too! Long dry stuff, that cracked almost as it bent down with the pressure of our bodies. ZIP! Ping! Ping! Zip! The gun flashes we could plainly see; rifle shots I knew, from the German lines. We hugged the edge of a large shell hole and waited a minute or so. Then forward, side-by-side, yard by yard. Slow work now! We were expert crawlers – and as silent as the grave. Never a word did we speak. It was a touch here – a slight pressure there – or signals of 'advance', 'stop' or 'danger near'. My heart almost stops! What the h★★★ is it? Something squirmed beneath me. I was lying on it. Like sheet lightning I turned on my side. It was a big rat. A screech of relief – and it bounds off. Hell! That was a start.

RIPPING PAST

By the luminous dial on my timepiece – we were now 'on the trail' well over an hour – it was 1.45am. It was time we came up against the wire. Flash! Crack! A bullet ripped the night air – struck the barbed wire – and sailed away at an angle – but that shot told us we were very close to Jerry.

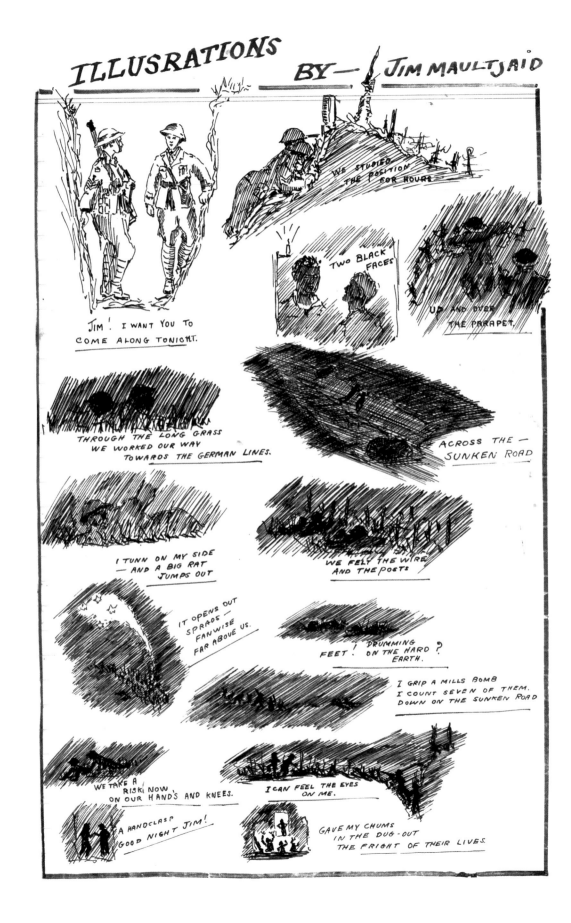

A THING OF BEAUTY – BUT

My sleeve catches on something! It's barbed wire. Now wire can be cruel. This piece was – it took a big bit of my sleeve away – and it left me with a severe scratch. We pause. My blood runs cold as the 'ting' of rusty spikes coming together sings like a clap of thunder in my ears. All is still. I compose myself. No sentry has been made suspicious. I breathe freely again. 'Hist!' Mr Wedgwood grips my arm. Up – straight up! – sails a coloured star shell – to burst in a blaze of tiny specks far above our heads. A thing of beauty – but not tonight. The click of the gun that shot it we plainly heard. Somehow I did not feel happy tonight, I was not my usual self, and had an uneasy feeling of something 'that was going to happen' or was I losing my nerve? I fight the feeling down (it is clearly recorded in my notes, written the very next day in the trenches that I had been out on patrol duty the night before and never felt so 'unhappy' as I did this night, on previous patrols).

THE STENCH WAS AWFUL

Along the German front line we wormed our way, down towards our left. We felt the posts. We handled the wires. We looked for the gaps, and noted the spaces left by our gunfire. Not a great deal of damage had been done, at least so far as we could see (or feel) and 'his' wire defences were in good order. The slight wind that was blowing wafted round to meet us in the face and the stench – that was almost unbearable – smote our nostrils. Bah! I almost choked, and clapped a hand across my mouth to keep it out. To cough here would be nearly fatal. With difficulty we restrained ourselves, and moved rapidly along to get clear of the affected zone. Was it an unburied body? We did not investigate!

BACK JIM! BACK!

'Let's go back Jim!' Close to my ear Lieutenant Wedgwood whispered, and I replied, 'Yes!' Slowly we veered around, and commenced the homeward track. My arms ached, my neck was stiff from the crawling position of the body for the last two hours or so, but my heart was glad – we were getting back.

CLOSER! … CLOSER! …

What's that! I pause. Voices. Yes, low sounds of muttered words reached our ears. Were they British? Or German? We flattened out, our ears close to the hard earth. The sound of many feet 'drumming' on the sun-baked soil came to us – closer! closer! … and closer! Germans without a doubt! 'My God! We are in for it now.' Now … I take a Mills from my breast pocket, let the pin drop out and raise my body a little – ready to throw, if discovered, and no escape seemed possible. They came straight for us! I knew that my companion had his revolver out – we were going to fight. No capture for us. Not ten yards away now. They stopped, all crouching. Were we discovered? My arm moved backwards – ready to throw. Swish! … rush! … swish … I ducked deeper into the clay. A rocket from the German front line rushed up above us! It soared into the black sky – it opened – spread out fanwise, bright as day, and dropped into our barbed wire, and they stood, revealed to us. I counted seven! But all had their backs to us, crouching down, on The Sunken Road. The flare died down. It was darker than ever. And they were gone!

Cold sweat broke out on me. My brow was damp! What a narrow escape! 'Phew!' gasps Mr Wedgwood. 'Close one that, Jim?' 'By the holy Smoke, Sir, it was!' 'Come on let's move in – I've had enough tonight.' In a relief I almost forgot the missing pin from the bomb and it was with a start of surprise that it dawned on me I was still holding this little iron 'death dealer' in a cramped right hand. A slip of the fingers – off goes the handle – then two more that would have never returned.

What would I do with it? Throw it and let it explode, or hold on until we got safely in? We couldn't have far to go now, so I'll hold on; besides if we bump into any more enemy patrols, it may be useful.

THOSE EYES

We got up on our hands and knees now – taking a risk, but anxious to get in. Our wire – welcome wire – was reached. No way through. We moved carefully along, found a spot that appeared to be thin. Stood up and worked cautiously forward. I could 'feel' the eyes on me! A safety catch snapped back. I cried out, 'Steady chum.' 'Who are you?' 'Night patrol,' we answered and whispered 'the password is …' 'All right! Come on.' We moved in – a bayonet almost touched my chest. That sentry was not quite satisfied yet. A good man, suspicious and very much on guard. We crouched on the parapet. 'It's Lieutenant Wedgwood and Sergeant Maultsaid.' 'Jump in!' And we slid down. With the bump down, I almost lost my grip on the bomb – that blasted bomb; that would have been three on the 'gone West' list.

SCARED FACES

'Goodnight Jim!' A hand clasp, and we go different ways.

I almost gave my chums in the dug-out a fit when I appeared in the candlelight with a blackened face.

THE GOLDEN IMAGE.

WOULD I TAKE IT ?

A Mystery …

How he came to have it in his possession was a mystery. It was shortly before the Battle of the Somme and we were lying in the woods behind Theipval, out for a short rest.

I knew he had something on his mind for some time back. Of a very jolly nature, this man had of late turned quiet and reserved, but then most of us had our own worries in these days – death was never far away – in fact it was often 'round the corner'. Still it was not like him to brood much on this matter – at least outwardly.

SERGEANT! SPARE ME A MINUTE

One evening, long after 'lights out' had gone, Private R. came quietly to my side and whispered 'Sergeant, would you come out a little bit with me? It's a very urgent private affair!' 'What's wrong old man?' I asked. 'I can't tell you here. Sergeant, won't you just spare me fifteen minutes or so?' 'All right! my lad. Hold on a minute.' Hastily I donned a few bits of clothing and my big overcoat. Through the dark wood we made our way. We came to a halt beneath a big tree, some five or six hundred yards from our resting place. A spot far from preying eyes or listening ears! *What the devil does he want to tell me*, I kept on wondering? *Has he murdered a chum, or did he intend to desert* – and wanted my advice?

I'M GOING, SERGEANT!

'Sergeant, I'm going to be killed!' I was startled! Now I had it. I was to take a record of his last wishes, et cetera. 'Nonsense!' I replied, 'you mustn't talk like that.'

'But I know it! I can feel it in me. I am not happy.' 'Look here, old man,' I said, as I put my arm on his shoulder. 'That's all in God's hands – and we must leave it at that.' His faith was not mine, but he nodded and said 'I know, I know, – but … but … wait!'

WHERE IN THE NAME?

'Strike a match, Sergeant.' I took out a box, and struck a light.

'What's this?' I gasped. It shone out a dull golden colour in the glare of the flame. Gold! Solid gold – without a doubt, and in the form of a crucifix.

'Where in the name of G★★ did you get this?' 'I got it … I got it … I got it at … it doesn't matter where I got it, – but Sergeant, for God's sake take it from me and take a burden from my shoulders.' 'No! No! No! I would have nothing to do with it. Why should I take it? Not for a million pounds would I have any dealings with this.'

'What'll I do with it?' 'I'm blessed if I know. Throw it away.' He would not do that. 'Keep it for luck.' He would not agree. 'Why did you take it?' 'Sorry is the day I did – I've never had a minute's peace of mind since.' I had a brainwave! 'What about digging a hole and burying it?'

'Yes! By G★★, that's a good idea.' He was relieved. I knew it. I could only dimly see his form in the overpowering darkness of the forest but, somehow, I knew he was pleased. I could feel it.

BURIED IN THE WOOD

'Here! Strike another match, and give me your entrenching spade.' I took his spade, picked a spot in the ground that felt soft – and dug a hole about a foot or so deep.

A strange scene this. But all was silence in this dark world of tall trees and swaying branches. He dropped it in. We shovelled in the loose earth. We stamped on it. I gathered some loose dead branches and covered the new earth. It was gone, gone forever, from our sight.

OUR SECRET

'Sergeant, you will never give me away?' 'No, chum, it's our secret.' I felt for his hand – and shook it.

'Are you happy now?' I asked. 'No! Sergeant, I'll never be forgiven. I'm going and going to … TO DIE … I KNOW IT.'

And he died. On 1 JULY 1916.

WE TOIL—
LIKE NAVVIES
INFANTRYMEN ONE WEEK
"NAVVIES" THE NEXT

NO rest for the troops. It was now the month of June. Days were long, and the ground as hard as iron. Great activity was apparent everywhere: in the air, on the ground, and under the ground too.

GUNS – MEN – AND MORE …

Guns, ammunition, men – then more! Day and night, battalions of infantry on the move. Day and night, the guns were moving up. Loads of all sizes of shells passed by. Dumps of trench boards, props, bombs, bully-beef, barbed wire, iron stakes, bags for filling in – in fact all the thousand and one requirements for modern war – and attack!

SOMETHING BIG IN THE WIND

Anyone with half an eye could tell there was something big in the wind. We were going – yes! going to attack! It was no 'latrine yarn' this time – it was the truth, and we looked forward to 'the day', that day on which we could get a smack at that, up to now, almost invisible enemy. My, that would be fine! Miserable days – and nights – were forgotten. That long dreary winter of 1915-16 had passed away like a nightmare, and soon the Ulster Division boys were to move forward. Hurrah! Hurrah! Hurrah!

NAVVY-SOLDIERS

In the line last week – out the next – but never more than several kilos from the battle area.

It was working parties now in relays. We never ceased. All day long – and all night through it was work! work! work! Labour, or pioneer battalions were scarce – these were the days of 'navvy soldiers'. Had troops, fighting troops, ever worked as we did in those hectic June days?

THE BLUE SKY – ABOVE

The 14th Royal Irish Rifles had not had a roof over their heads for weeks past. God's pure air and sky were ours; brown and tanned, to a deep, deep red, we looked the picture of health. Yes! we were in fighting trim!

'Sergeant Maultsaid! Take your section and report at ****** for digging gunpits, and report to Sergeant so and so, Royal Engineers.' Off we went at 9.00pm, rifles and shovels (what a contrast?) 'Here you are boys!' Four big, ugly, short-nosed monsters stood on the roadside. 'Dig four pits here, and here.' The ditch was soon attacked. We dug deep into the chalk sides of this road, all in the darkness of night – and the 'war' was not very far away. Star shells flashed – night fell deeper. A few lonely shells sang away over, far above us – and we took a breather. Finished! 'Right away my lads!' We trudged home, tired, sore, and sleep weary.

BURDENS OF THE WIRE!

Up the road we toiled. Single file, every man burdened with the big rolls of barbed wire. Cursed stuff this! Each side of us the forest looked cool and comfortable. 'Can we fall out, Sergeant?' 'Yes. Have a few minutes, but no smoking.' 'Come along now boys! Let's get this d*** stuff up, and get back as soon as possible.'

Swish! S–w–i–s–h–! … over it came. We did not hesitate. Down went wire, bodies and all. Crash!

Pieces of metal clattered down. We waited a few seconds, gathered ourselves, and our cargo – then proceeded.

THE CLINK OF A SHOVEL

Little bogie trucks are filled up. Chalk, clay, rubbish all shovelled in – then the little truck is pushed down the line, out into the swamp. We were actually building a road across now. It was night time again. We were careful as the sky lit up every few minutes with ours and, more often, Jerry's star rockets. Sound travels rapidly at night. The clink of a shovel against the iron body of a truck sounds … well!, it sounded like a thunderclap in our ears.

Hour after hour we toiled. The first streaks of dawn lit up the sky away beyond the wood – and then zirr –zirr –zip! zip! zip! A machine gun crashed out. We flattened out.

The art of 'getting down to it' was now a side line. Crawling out of the path of danger, we gathered our squad together. I looked them over, and we slid away through the trees, back for a rest, and a cup of warm tea. Another night had gone!

A CHALLENGE FOR JERRY

Nights were disturbed now. The gun flashes came from unsuspected quarters. Quiet all day, these fiends barked out their challenge to the Hun at night. It was getting hotter each night, and we never seemed to get quite clear of it. Day and night, it was a case of 'always on the spot'. We toiled. We broiled, and then toiled again. Very little rest now – but the spirit of the lads never faltered. It was all in the day's work, and we were all volunteers. Of course we groused! That was our safety valve, for letting off steam. We cursed the war. We cursed all kinds of things, and people, we asked: what did they take us for? Navvies? And yet … we carried on.

IN OUR MIND'S EYE

Sometimes we sang songs – songs that meant just nothing at all – soldiers' songs. A song about the 'Old County Down', or 'The Hills of Donegal' would bring a lump to our throats. The mind's eye went back over the sea, to the old homeland; we could see it all again – our young boyhood days. Would we ever be boys again? Or the face of a loved one would creep out from the trees and stand mirrored before us. We looked back … back … back.

STEEL HAT—GAS MASK
AMMUNITION—RIFLE
EQUIPMENT—PICK AND
SHOVEL. THE SOLDIER of
THE GREAT WAR

SOMETHING NEW —
— IN GUNS
BARK!
BOOM! BOOM!

JIM MAULTSAID

LIKE a thief in the night 'it' came. Our slumbers were disturbed in a shattering way one fine summer's night.

What new mode of night horror was this? It was not a 'boom'. It was a 'bark', like a mighty whip. It cut the night air with an earsplitting crash! We were curious of course. Its approach, we knew, by the puff, puff, of an engine on the railway line, then much hub-bub, and crash of a huge shell being launched into the sky. Half a dozen explosions, then the little engine clanked away again, and the night's work was over.

I WATCHED
Several nights of this got the better of my curiosity and I got up one dark night, crawled down to the edge of the railway embankment – and watched the proceedings.

FLASH! CRACK!
I could not, of course, see too well, but the flash of the shells gave me a fair idea of this 'strafe'.

Below me in a big iron truck sat a long-nosed monster with its big barrel pointing towards the German front. Little figures flitted around – the gunners. Each explosion almost lifted my head off, and the earth trembled. A squat black engine of powerful build sat quite near; this was the means of movement. It was a great idea: a travelling gun, not new I suppose, but good enough to let the enemy have a dose of 'heavy stuff', then clear out.

SEARCHING FOR US

The boys did not fancy this 'carry on' a great deal – coming so close to our resting place in the woods – as after several nights' 'strafing' the German long-range batteries started to search for our big fellow.

I think the enemy tumbled to our little game as one fine day a shower of 'heavies' came rushing over and left the railway line in a mess. It was like a pepper duster, all cut in holes – and stopped our 'gunplay' from this particular spot that night.

Of course, as usual, the PBI got the job of repairing the damage. A rail squad went into action when darkness came down. Picks, shovels, bigger sleepers, and rails were hauled around, and during the patching up of this the working party was scattered to the four winds several times by blasts of enemy shell fire. What a b***** war? Who the h*** took us for railway men? H*** roast that d*** gun! May the d*** thing blow up some night! The language was 'hot stuff' that particular night. After all, the boys had cause to grouse. Why should the fighting-line troops be always called out to make good the damage when we really should have been getting very much needed sleep, after a hard day's work on some fatigue or other.??????? THAT GUN WAS UNPOPULAR.

AS you can see from the little cutting below taken from 'the book', each time we took over duty in the front-line trenches it was 'hotter' than the last one!

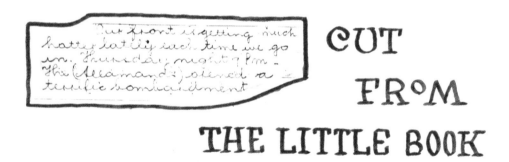

CUT FROM THE LITTLE BOOK

STIRRING EVENTS FORESHADOWED

Stirring events were in the very air itself. There was going to be a big 'blaze up' at no distant date. The boys knew it – and the enemy knew it too!

THE 'GROWL' OF THE GUNS

All day long the guns boomed. All day long the air was filled with the planes from both sides, and the hours of darkness were made hideous by the growling of artillery.

Away to our right, and left, we could hear the thunder of the guns! Just one long 'growl' from sunset till sunrise. Coming events casting their shadows before?

Little clumps of trees by the roadside actually spitting flame! Old houses glowing red hot, then lighting up the sky! Hurling death and destruction from every conceivable vantage

28

point. An innocent looking bit of green foliage hiding several big monsters of guns. The sides of a sunken road could fall away, and in your view would be revealed scores of light field guns. Guns! Guns! Guns!

WE ARE STARTLED

Marching down the road in silence. Flash! Crash! Crash! Your very eardrums were almost shattered as a whole battery let loose, almost at your feet, to startle your heart into terrific activity – and send the blood thundering into your brain. It took several seconds to compose yourself.

UNDERESTIMATED

Our artillery men made one little error, and that was that they were too confident. They told us again and again that nothing could live against this hurricane of shellfire. We would find out later that something did live indeed – very much alive and kicking. But then we did not know how deeply the enemy had 'dug in'; we found this out after paying an awful price for the discovery. You will read the story later when you turn to the pages of my description of the 1 July Battle.

DIGGING IN! – AND OUT!

Did the Germans sit and take our bombardments without reply? Not likely! They hit back – and hit d★★★ hard too, as you may well believe. Of course, through all these hectic days and nights, the poor old infantry man went in – into 'Hell'. We were blown up – blown down – blown sideways – and all ways. Digging in! Digging out! And then all over again. Ah! It was murder! How our nerves stood the strain, the Lord only knows!

BLOW THEM TO H★★★

I looked out from a point of observation, and I saw the German front line on fire. Pleased? By the 'holy Smoke' I was delighted. A bit of our own back at last! Man! It's great. Blow them to H★★★ yelled 'Kid Lewis'. 'Blow the b★★★★★★★ to H★★★,' screeched 'Father McBride'. We remembered our past ordeals, our sufferings, and my blood boiled up. 'Yes! Knock blazes out of them,' I shouted – shouted to our gunners, who were miles behind us. What did we care? They must have heard us – as before our eyes – yes! – our very eyes up – up in the air, sky high, went yards of the Hun front line. Cheers!

THE FIRST ROUND

The gloves were off now!
All out for the 'knockout'.

THREE IN! FOUR TO GO?

Tree trunks, shattered and split, fell around us. The ground was rocking, swaying, reeling.

Lumps of chalk flew past, bits of barbed wire spun past. Pieces of the wood and sandbags went up in clouds of black smoke. The Earth trembled. The world (this world of ours) was crashing around us! Bullets 'zizzed' like angry bees – to sink with a sickening thud into a tree stump. Black ugly tree stumps stuck up, all about us – like devils mocking us in our misery.

'We are getting it now.'

'We have been getting the same thing for days past.' How many more have we to 'do' until relieved?

Three in – and four to go?

I cannot say! My mind is fogged.

NERVES ON EDGE.

Nerves on edge, we go through, as if in a dream! Can it really all be true? Or, a nightmare that will pass away in a little while?

FULL BROTHER TO THE STOKES

Our trench mortar batteries were now a strong feature of 'strafe' for the Germans. This was a gun that spat out bombs the size of footballs and they exploded like a clap of thunder. Fearsome things – no doubt – but the funny thing again to the mind of the infantry man was: these squads shot half a dozen bombs over from a certain section of front-line trench, then moved away some several hundreds of yards to leave us sitting, just waiting on Jerry's reply. Good enough!

This was a full brother to the Stokes gentleman – and about as popular.

JIM. MAULTSAID.

WE ARE GETTING IT HOTTER –

– EACH TIME WE COME IN

AND OUR ARTILLERY IS PLAYING THE DEVIL WITH THE GERMAN LINES

A VIEW FROM OUR TRENCHES OF JERRYS FRONT LINE

A STRANGE OUTFIT. BIG BOMBS THE SIZE OF FOOTBALLS

— DRAWN BY JIM MAULTSAID —

HERE SHE COMES ...!

Phut! Phut! I guess they are at it now. 'Look out boys!' We anxiously scan the space between us and the German front line. 'Down boys! Here she comes!' And by G★★ 'She' came. Crash! Crash!

WISH I HAD JOINED THE REs

Mighty trench shells fall on us! The black smoke clears. Our wire has a gap ten yards wide.

'What the hell brings that bunch of 'Yahoos' here, with their d★★★★★ gun?' We rant, and rave, and curse. Hail, rain, or sunshine, shells or no shells – we cannot leave our posts. That's the fellow called 'infantry of the line'. 'Wish I had joined the engineers,' sighs Rooney!

A SONG OF JOY – AND FREEDOM

A bird sings its joy of life away high up above us. We listen – and we envy it – its freedom!

LITTLE WHITE PUFFS

Little white puffs of smoke against the blue of a perfect summer sky far up in the heavens attract my attention. Forgetting my own worries, I stare up long and intently at the little puffs chasing a fighting plane of ours. It was ours, I knew from the shape of it – and the drone of his engine, we could tell the difference now – friend or foe.

He was far out over the German lines. I fell to wondering, would he ever return? Brave fellows – these boy airmen of ours. We admired their nerve – and fighting spirit!

GAS! GAS! FROM US

A WASH OUT

THE GAS SQUAD are sending their stuff across today! Who, and what, was this lot of gentry? We stand back and wonder! Strange cylinders, nozzles and contraptions pass by – the rarest collection of men it was my privilege to see during my travels. Were they soldiers – or what?

Somehow, I had very little faith in their ability to 'deliver the goods'; they were anything but impressive. Of course, as usual, we had to carry most of their outfit up the trenches to the scene of operations. Thank the Lord – we had not to stand by and assist them – they could gas away there to their hearts' content. 'And what happens?' says Kelly, 'if the shell drops in around the cylinder Sergeant?' 'Search me old man! Let them alone.' 'What way is the wind blowing now,' whispers Rogers! Kid Lewis pulls a long face and says, 'It's blowing straight into us!' Gas helmets are examined eagerly – it looks serious and we do not fancy being gas victims – from our own gas.

How the stunt worked out I cannot really say – but, from all the available information, this attempt to give Jerry some of his own medicine was a complete WASH OUT, much to our relief!

THE GAS SQUAD
IN ACTION

AS USUAL THE POOR INFANTRYMAN
BROUGAT UP "THE DOPE."

ALL PICTURES
BY
JIM.MAULSA

WHAT WAY
IS THE WIND
BLOWING NOW
WHISPERS
ROGERS
P.

WHAT HAPPENS SEGT
IF A SHELL LIGHTS
AMONGST THEM
SAYS -KELLY-

SUSPICIOUS PIGEONS.

I DID NOT LIKE THE LOOK OF HIM —— OR HIS PIGEONS

CASTING my memory back, the looks of this big Frenchman (?) did not appeal to me. The boys that served on the Somme front before 1 July 1916 no doubt can remember him strutting around Martinsart.

He lived in a very big house near the corner of the road that led up to the trenches on the side of the village facing the firing line, and a very high wall surrounded his place of abode.

WHY SO MANY PIGEONS?
One thing I did notice, and that was on the side of the house stood several pigeon boxes that appeared to contain scores of these birds. They cooed and fluttered about all day. They came and went.

WE WERE SLACK
If you expect me to tell you this man was a spy – and that we discovered him etc., etc. – well, you'll be sorely disappointed. But I often thought and reasoned: what is he here for? And as impertinent as could be! No love for the British troops, this son of France! Was he a Frenchie at all? Our people were slack in these kinds of things. He came, and went, in and out amongst the battalions at his own sweet will. Of course, I may be all wrong in my opinion of this black-bearded overbearing fellow that lived apparently all alone in a big house so near to the firing line. Yet, why did he stay there? It may be that he would not leave the town – or it may be that he had reasons for staying there. For my part I would have cleared him out at the double. No evidence against him, but every time our lot passed this way – I liked him less and less.

I DID NOT LIKE THE LOOK OF HIM

JIM MAULTSAID.

OR HIS HOUSE

BEHIND THE BIG WALL
AT THE JUNCTION OF
THE ROADS

PIGEON BOXES WERE PROMINENT

WAS HE THE
LORD MAYOR of
MARTINSART

?

I WOULD HAVE CHEERFULLY COMMANDED A FIRING SQUAD

EACH TIME HE PASSED
I LIKED HIM LESS—AND
—LESS

ALL PICTURES BY
JIM MAULTSAID.

WILLING TO ACT

Was he the Lord Mayor of the town? I do not know. But one thing I do know and that is if a firing squad had been required to put him against the wall I would have applied for the job of SERGEANT OF THE SQUAD.

'ALL RED'

THE TROOPS COULD NOT BELIEVE THEIR EYES!

CAN you believe it? An 'all red' machine! We were startled to see it swoop from the skies one summer's day. Was it a German? Did our eyes tell us the truth? Argument was fierce among the troops, but one point was soon settled: it was a German all too true, as several of our red, white and blue boys give chase at once. He came over at a good altitude and held a big advantage in this respect – and he led a troop of fighting planes after him. He was a 'leader'; we could easily see that – and a good one too! But all red – it was a novelty – and daring!

A FIGHT WE ENJOYED

Our squadron were now well up, and a fight looked like taking place. Would the Germans fight, or run?

'ALL RED'

We had not long to wait. They were at it, hammer and tongs. What a battle! In and out – sidestepping – looping the loop – stalling – diving – and shooting at each other. Like little ants up in the clouds.

We held our breath and strained our eyes, watching this life and death struggle thousands of feet above the earth's surface. It was one of the most thrilling air battles we had yet witnessed – and we were thrilled to our very boots! Which side would break up first? Jerry was stronger – having several more in numbers compared to us, – but our lads had nerve to tackle anything. The Hun machines appeared to have more speed – at least to us it looked that way.

HAND-TO-HAND – IN THE AIR

Not a shell burst interrupted them – the anti-aircraft gunners being afraid to fire. It was a real hand- to-hand battle of the air. The Red leader came in for a great deal of attention, but he was clever. How he ducked! How he shot straight down when almost cornered! Gee! He was a fire air bird. A bird that was hard to corner.

DOWN! DOWN!

Was the German formation breaking up? Yes! – By the holy Smoke we had them on the run.

Away they went – like a flock of black swans – back home – and our boys in hot pursuit. The all-red leader led the way.

I TURN SICK AT THE THOUGHT

A bright red flame flashes up! What is it? A German machine on fire. He staggers! Two of the British machines flash past him – pumping lead into his already blazing body – I suppose.

Then! Down! Down! Down! On fire. Like a streak of rushing fire flame he rushes to meet the earth to which he belongs – poor soul, his troubles are now over. He is already dead – I hope. My heart stopped beating! What a death! I turned sick at the thoughts of such an end – and he was young too, just a young German boy – fresh from school? All the airmen seemed to be in their early years of manhood.

OLD MOTHER EARTH FOR ME!

Bad enough down here. I certainly did not fancy the 'up in the air business'. No, Siree! The old mother earth, for James Maultsaid.

WRITTEN IN THE TRENCHES

JUNE 1916

Sometimes the old heart lost faith – but not for long.
Never mind! Never mind! Sadness today. Tomorrow – gladness!
A few lines from the 'little book': 'we wait for the word GO!'
'Confident – and ready to lay down our lives.'
The Ulster division, I know, will 'make a name for itself'.
The finest division that ever landed 'on foreign shores'.
'Boastful words – perhaps!'
Our motto – 'No Surrender!' handed down the ages, by Ulstermen to their sons.
Our faith in God, in ourselves – was immense.
No German troops existed – that could stop us. We would die in our tracks for the cause of civilisation.

FATEFUL HOURS

ALL READY FOR THE WORD

'GO BOYS'

WE knew that 'the day' was looming near. Like a bunch of schoolboys we'd looked forward to our great adventure. Honestly, not one out of the thousand would have missed this, the day we had been training for – for ages now! It was to be real 'warfare', not this hitting in the dark by unseen forces. What a chance to get a crack at the gentlemen that slung this 'dope' at us! Gee whizz! It was a glorious thought, and we waited! We had waited far too long already in my humble opinion. A REST FROM INFERNAL GUNS.

DIGGING OUR OWN

Brought back from the infernal roar of the guns, and the never-ending working squads, we really got a real rest, for a few days.

OUR LAST WORKING PARTY

What do you think our last fatigue was? Let me tell you. It was the digging of long narrow trenches from each side of Elgin Avenue in the wood. These were to be our 'stations' or the 'jumping off' points on the morning of the big attack. Narrow slits only. Not enough room to sit or lie down. In the white chalk we cut them out. One of the lads said it was our graves we were digging. How true that poor fellow was in making this joke! They certainly were – the only graves some of our poor souls ever knew. They never got further than this point on that fatal morn.

BE PREPARED!

I actually find an old French grindstone and put a point on my bayonet that would have done credit to a needle – and an edge that would have disgraced a razor. Horrible thoughts these now, after the years have passed away, but as this book is a true story I cannot do anything else but tell the truth. I was getting ready. War was war!

MUCH CLEANING

Rifles were taken to pieces – and cleaned. Bombs were examined carefully. Our ammunition was polished up – round by round – some two hundred and fifty cartridges in all. Nothing left to chance.

A MISTAKE?

Flags, on long thin poles to mark our extreme point of advance, were issued to us. Shovels were dished out also; these were to be stuck through our little haversacks on the back and carried into action. Another mistake in my opinion, this loading up of the fighting man. Our movements should have been free and easy. Imagine a bomber, such as I was, hampered with a heavy pick, dozens of bombs, a rifle, equipment, and hundreds of rounds of ammunition? The bombers, especially, should not have been asked to carry pick or shovel I may tell you now. We soon found this out – and 'dumped' the lot! The shovels and picks, I mean, as we simply could not throw bombs with this stuff on our backs.

A GENTLEMAN

LIEUTENANT P. WEDGWOOD 14TH ROYAL IRISH RIFLES (YCV)

DIED 1 July 1916, as a gallant gentleman would – facing the foe. One of my best and dearest friends his 'passing on' was a terrible blow to me; you can read the story of his death in my article 'July 1st 1916'. We had faced dangers in no man's land side by side, knowing and understanding each other as few men do: on duty my platoon officer; off duty I was just 'Jim'. Of a frail build, yet a heart like a lion; it was a great adventure to him and even after all these years I can see his smile as it slowly crept around the corners of his mouth. The boys of his platoon had a nickname for him – 'The Prince' – but he held a big spot in their hearts and his orders were faithfully carried out. Sad to relate, his brother was also killed on the same date – a terrible blow to his parents. Such is war – and the price. GOD REST HIS SOUL.

PICTURE PAGE.

I COMMENCE A TORNADO ATTACK

HERE YOU SEE AN ARMY OPEN AIR BOXING DISPLAY SOMEWHERE IN FRANCE.

ALL READY FOR THE BATTLE IN THE LIGHTWEIGHT CHAMPIONSHIP JUNE 1916

109 BRIGADE SPORTS

ON THE VERY EVE OF THE BIG PUSH WE HOLD A SPORTS DAY – THAT WAS THE SPIRIT OF THE TROOPS

I BOX FOR THE CHAMPIONSHIP. I WIN THE ONE HUNDRED YARDS.
THE 14TH WIN A RELAY.

THE INNISKILLINGS ARE GREAT SPORTSMEN

WAR FORGOTTEN
OWING to some alteration in the timetable of our commanders in chief, the 'big push' was put back several days. We were at a loose end. Why not a sports meeting? No sooner thought of than it was duly arranged. Orders flashed from Brigade HQ. It had to be done – and done it was: 109 Brigade will hold a sports meeting. Worried platoon sergeants raked in the entries for Boxing, Running, Bombing competitions etc., etc. No shortage from the YCVs. We entered in dozens.

THE USUAL
The fatigue squads were called into action (they always were) and a boxing ring erected in a hollow – out in the open – real American! Running tracks were measured out, and all the usual preparations duly carried out for a big day's fun.

SKINS Vs RIFLES
It would be impossible for me to give you a full report of this programme, so I shall confine myself more or less to the events I took a part in, large or small.

The competitors were all from the 9th, 10th and the 11th Inniskillings and of course the 14th Rifles (YCV).

SERGEANT MAULTSAID Vs CORPORAL ********?
Sorry I cannot remember his name, but he was from the Skins. We were drawn in the lightweight class. First contest.

The sun beats down. Crowded around the ring were thousands of 'fans', all eager to cheer their own hope to victory. Gloves adjusted, my seconds give me a final rub. Time!

Out like a Flash – I carry the fight to my opponent. He was slow. Oh! So slow! I knew I had him. My only trouble was keeping clear of his big wild swings. A poor fighter. Round after round. I plastered him. Four 3-minute rounds – and I won by a mile.

A CORPORAL AGAIN

CORPORAL Vs – SERGEANT MAULTSAID
Again I meet one of the Skins' and a Corporal too! His name I forget. This was my second fight.

He was a tough lad, heavy, and he carried a wicked left. I fought a cool battle – and piled up the points, to score a handsome victory. Going well now for the championship. This was the semi-final bout.

How the 14th men yelled! 'Get in Jim!' 'Keep at him Sergeant!' And I sure did.

FOR THE TITLE NOW

SERGEANT MAULTSAID Vs CORPORAL

I had him!

I was exhausted. The last battle had taken it out of me, a great deal. My seconds worked like slaves. I feel better now. Across the ring I take a look at my opponent. A sturdy young man. 'Can you lick him Jim?' Jimmy Magee whispers. 'Shure! I can, Jim – just wait!'

The bell sounds. I bound out. We shake hands – then the fight of my career begins. Ducking, swaying, punching – at a terrific pace. It's a fierce affray. I feel confident. Not once has he landed a blow on me. Round two. Across that square I simply bounded – to crash home a straight left, followed by a right hook. My fighting blood was up! And I had him! I knew I had him! Round three. My strength was slowly going – but I bluffed, and fought as I never did before. We mixed it – he was still strong. Not a mark on me yet – and I had his face covered with blood. 'You'll win easy, Jim!' Round 4, and last; now for it. We shake hands. Bang! Bang!

I commence a tornado attack. He gives ground. Bah! I run into a wild right-hand swing – and take it on the nose. Blood! I'm smothered in it.

I can hear the roar of the crowd in my ears. Like the sea. Throwing all the boxing ability I ever possessed to the winds, I attack! Attack! Attack! Red mists float before my eyes.

I smash blows from all angles at the face before me. I fight like a wildcat. 'Come on Jim! Come on boy! Sock him! Sock him!' A supreme effort – I make it a hurricane finish.

The bell goes. Time!

A deep silence falls.

I WAS DECLARED – THE LOSER

GROANS! CAT CALLS!

I can hardly believe it yet – how I was counted as LOSER. It was a 'raw' deal – but such is sport. The decision was badly, very badly, received – shouts of no! no! and groans.

I was astounded. If ever I won a fight, I won this one. Still! It's all in the game. Strange to say, I heard afterwards that all my three opponents this day fell on 1 July 1916!

TWO HUNDRED FRANCS RICHER

Field events came next. I had by now got over my ill-luck feeling, and was the richer by some two hundred francs for my three fights. Not a bad day's work (about £10 in English cash), this was a small fortune in those days as our pay was small – very, very small indeed.

RED HOT RIVALS

The inter-battalion rivalry was red hot in all the track races. Our most dangerous opponents were the Derry boys (10th Inniskillings).

NED KELLY – CHAMPION

How pleased I was to see my crack bomb thrower 'Ned' Kelly annex the First Prize for throwing. Over fifty yards he could throw – and get the target! My! He was class. Good old YCVs – and No. 14 Platoon – went wild.

'JIM! I CAN BEAT YOU'

Heats in the hundred yards were run off in between. I was afraid to get into the same heat as my full cousin DOT MAULTSAID (Junior International footballer and all round sportsman) of the 10th (Derry) Inniskillings. By good luck we missed each other. We both ran out winners in our heats – and must meet in the final.

'Jim! I can beat you today! I'm in great form.' Dot will have his joke. 'No! My boy – this is my day out,' I replied.

THE TROOPS INVEST

The 100 yards final. Line up! The bell rings. I feel great. 'Can you win Sergeant?' Several of my platoon are very anxious. They have, I'm afraid been putting the francs down. 'Don't worry boys – I'll win alright!'

RUNNING FOR LIFE – AND THE YCVs

Crack! We are off! The flash of that revolver was my signal. I almost beat the report – and I'm running as I never ran before, 30 – 20 – 10 yards to go – I lead.

A mighty effort – and I carried tape yards away, in my last supreme burst – to WIN THE 100 YARDS DASH – FOR THE YCVs

BILLY SCOTT

A FAMOUS 'MILER'

We rest on the grass. A hot summer day, and watch our chums in the mile. I cannot remember if the 14th won, or not, but I think it fell to a Sergeant Billy Scott, a famous 'miler' from Ulsterville, and a champion. (He fell, poor soul, in the war at a later date.)

AND THE RELAY

RELAY TEAMS get ready. This was an event we were very keen to win. It was an affair of honour, 'for the Regiment', our Regiment.

The team to represent the YCVs was POWELL, KELLY, MULHOLLAND and MAULTSAID.

All smart sprinters and, again, we feared the Derry lads.

A TERRIFIC RACE

Excitement was at fever pitch as the first four lined up.

Get ready! Set! Crack! Off they go.

Down the course 220 yards sped these four lads, straining every ounce of strength and energy to get a lead. Alfie Mulholland represents us – he's going fine. Alfie, at his best, could move some – and by heavens he moved this day – to hand over the baton – several yards in the lead from his nearest rival.

Away goes 'Kelly'. A long legged, long striding runner, he holds on to our lead – indeed he increases it.

We still hold our advantage as Ernie Powell snatches the stick to flash down the track. But Ernie's opponent is a good lad – he gains ground. We fret and foam as he slowly draws level. All our advantage has 'gone west' practically. Here they come. I gather myself for the 'get away' and I'm off.

It was a race of 220 yards – as a sprint – pure murder.

Halfway round I was leading, but not for long. Looming up beside me is Quartermaster Sergeant Dot Maultsaid of the Skins. He pants out, 'I have you now Jim!' I did not reply – breath was too precious. The crowd roar! D Company can be heard miles away. 'Come on D. Come on! Come on!' Did I hear them? Yes! I certainly did. I have been running neck and neck, but could not get a lead.

Rounding the last corner, then down the straight for home. I see the crowd clustered around the winning post.

This is my objective.

All my reserve strength is called up. I'm going to win – or die!

Arms flying, heart beating a thousand to the minute, I strain – and gain inches, to hurl my body past the post – TO WIN THE RELAY CHAMPIONSHIP.

Dot Maultsaid was granted a commission in the field, and was killed on a raiding party later in the war. He died, as he had lived, a GENTLEMAN.

DERRY FOOTBALLER MISSING.

Second-Lieutenant W. MAULTSAID.

Second-Lieutenant Wesley Maultsaid, Royal Irish Rifles, who has been reported wounded and missing, is a native of Derry, where many of his relatives reside. He is a well-known footballer, and while plying for the Derry Institute Club was selected to represent his country in a Junior International contest. He joined the Army since the outbreak of war, and received his commission on the field. Second-Lieutenant Maultsaid is brother of Mr. Arthur Maultsaid, Glengormley, Belfast, and the continued absence of news concerning his fate or whereabouts is giving much anxiety.

✳ KILLED IN ACTION
NOV 12TH 1916.

THE BATTLE IN NO-MANS-LAND

WHEN RIVAL PATROLS MET
— BY JIM MAULTSAID. —

PICTURE FROM "THE REAL LIFE" DAYLIGHT RAID

JULY 1ˢᵗ 1916

GLORIOUS CHARGE BY THE 36ᵗʰ ULSTER DIVISION. WE STORM THIEPVL RIDGE. SUCCESS AND FAILURE. BUT NO — SURRENDER.

WE MOVE FORWARD TO BATTLE.

THE sun has gone down. We stand to arms. All is in readiness for our last trip to the assembly trenches. We 'go over' the top tomorrow – at dawn.

Chums in different companies have been paid their last visit – all is now business – and the little village of Léalvillers will soon see the end of the 14th Rifles (YCVs).

BY THE RIGHT- QUICK MARCH!

'Fall in! Right dress! Number! Move to the right – in fours! Form fours! Right! By the right – quick march! Eyes left!' The commanding officer sits on his horse – and salutes each platoon – as we swing past. He gives us a word of cheer. I feel both elated – and sad.

What does fate hold in store for me? We move forward in battle formation, full of life – and hope.

Old familiar spots are passed on this fateful journey. Conversation is carried on, in an undertone, as we tramp along. Boom! Boom! Boom! Dull sounds, away up in the front, tell us that the heavy guns are lashing themselves into a fury pounding the German lines – to help us.

GUNNERS! BLOODY RED

Martinsart again! Down the street well known to us we tramp. Halt! Packs off! The old pack is unbuckled, and dumped – all in a heap. Light battle order now. No time is lost – we again move on, down through the path by the wood.

The order comes through 'single file'. Into the wood now, a forest of many memories to me: Aveluy wood. The trees stand tall silent sentinels, and watch us pass.

Crash! Crack! Crash! Crack! Crack! Crash! Hell! Yes! Hell let loose; all the guns we possess seem to be around these parts tonight crashing out a mighty challenge to the Hun.

Not a moment's respite now. That din swells into a roar – long growing, and ear splitting. Gunners stripped to the waist look bloody red as the flashes from the explosions light up the darkness of a summer's night. All straining, sweating, and cursing as they slam home shells of all sizes into the breaches of those almost human monsters of war.

War! Hellish war!

Into the communication trench – almost at our destination now – in the Thiepval wood.

NO REST

Whizz – bang! Whizz – bang!

Whizz – bang! Whizz – bang!

No.14 Platoon almost 'goes West'. Down into the chalk we dive, on top of each other, all of a jumble.

God! Those four shells almost took my breath away. They crashed right on the top of the parapet. Out in the open we would have been blown to atoms. The boys crush up from the rear, and we stagger forward. Nothing must hold up the troops. A deadly start this to our adventure!

The wood is a mass of flame. Shells bursting, trees crashing; all is confusion, and din. A din that shocks the eardrums. A din that puts trying to talk to your nearest chum out of all consideration.

We stagger on – then turn right.

Crouching down, we pass into our assembly trench to rest for the night, awaiting the dawn.

We cannot rest. It's impossible. You cannot sit, lie down. Just stand up, and wait. Slowly the night hours pass away. Hours of torture – and misery. My thoughts race round and round. Home! Loved ones! And the future! Would I lose an arm? Or a leg? Or both? God save me from the loss of my sight! I dreaded blindness! Ah! Anything but that. What was Heaven really like?

Would I meet my dear old mother up there, once again? Yes! I would. It gives me great calmness! I'm not afraid now. Why should I fear death? A little pocket Bible rests in my breast pocket, right over my heart. Watches are now looked at every few minutes. Nearly 6.00am. We take a final look at our bombs, and rifles.

THE LAST HOUR

The air is rent with a tornado of gunfire – the last hour. Hurricane shelling now. Jerry is on the jump. He fears the dawn too! His guns make reply to ours. Are we really coming? Surely 'hell' is no more or no less than this?

GOODBYE OLD CHUM

Lieutenant Monard's voice startles me, 'Have some rum Jim?' 'No sir!' I refuse. We shake hands, and say no more. 'Sergeant, if I go out here's my address. Will you call and tell them?' 'Shure! Old man! I'll do that.' This, a request from a pal. Goodbye old chum: God take care of you.

'Come on boys,' Lieutenant S. Monard yells. We follow. Up, and over the rough trench ladders into the shell-shattered wood. Across a wooden gangway over our front-line trench and we are out into no man's land.

CRACK-RAT-TAT—ZIP-ZIP.BOOM!

A wall of flame meets us. We stagger, and gasp from shock. My very hair seems to scorch under the impact. The air is full of hissing, burning metal, and the ground rocks beneath our feet as we tear our way through our own wire defences.

At last! At last! We are attacking. Boom! Boom! Crash! Crack! Rat – tat – tat – zip – zip – zip. How the bullets sing past – like angry bees. Clouds of black smoke blind us. My eyes smart. What is the sweet smelling stuff? Tear gas shells?

WE SURGE FORWARD

'Close up boys. Keep your line!' I yell. We surge forward, across that blackened shell-bleached strip of ground. Steady, as if on parade, those boys of ours faced a fire that was simply 'hell'.

The sun shines down on us. Bayonets sparkle and glint.

Cries, and curses, rend the air. Chums fall, some without a sound – and others? Oh! My God may I never hear such cries again. There goes the YCV flag tied to the muzzle of a rifle. That man had nerve.

BRAVO! THE INNISKILLINGS

Through the smoke, just ahead of us, after we had crossed the sunken road (a road of misery and pain) we could see khaki figures rushing the German front line.

The Inniskillings had got at them. Wild Irish yells floated to our ears. We quicken our pace. We want to help.

HERE THEY COME

Here comes Jerry! Out to meet us? Yes! But – hands held high above their heads. Haggard, worn out, wild-eyed beings. Shell-shocked and battered. What they suffered during our hurricane of bombardment the Lord only knows.

Line after line of brown figures press on, and on. Gaps are filled.

What a glorious sight! The enemy had now set up a terrible barrage of shell-fire, and machine guns were hammering out a deadly stream of death-dealing messengers. Big gaps appeared, but nothing on this earth could have stopped those Ulster boys – their Irish blood aflame, thirsting to get 'close in'.

Advance! Advance! We cannot stop to help the wounded. The order is – forward!

Tis' said that some of the Skins wore Orange sashes rushing the Germans, shouting 'No Surrender'. It's true too. A finer lot of men never lived. How they fought! Like madmen. Honour and glory for their famous regiment.

IN! IN! Amongst them

Dashing into the German front-line trench system that, in parts, had been battered to destruction by our gunfire – in other sections it was intact – we stumbled in amongst the wreckage of bodies, wooden beams, and revetments. Few living 'Huns' here to stay our progress.

BLOOD! BLOOD! BLOOD!

My work commences! My squad were detailed to clear out the dug-outs. On reaching the German front line I had noticed that we had been suffering heavy losses, and nearly all the boys that had fallen had been shot through the right side (from the direction of Thiepval village). A nest of snipers or a machine gun had been missed. This news I shouted to Mr Wedgwood of 15 Platoon. 'Come on Jim! Let's clear them out.' Rapid orders to my bombing section, and we at once attacked, by turning right, down the trench. Corner to corner. Shell hole to shell hole. We rushed, and closed in on the troublesome spot. A battle royal takes place. We fight a little war – all on our own. Rifle and bomb comes into play. Our lads have been thinned down. Several good fellows have fought their last fight.

A head appears. A rifle. I take rapid aim. Crack! Two arms cleave the air. A big German jumps up from a trench, hurls a bomb. Crash! My God! Mr Wedgwood is gone … gone … gone. I see red! Blood! Blood! Blood! My breast bursts with anger. I rise and rush straight at the German bomber. He rises up to meet me. His rifle jumps to his shoulder, to shoot. Quick as a flash, I hurl a Mills bomb, shattering flame around his face. A lifeless trunk slides back into the trench, and I slide in, on top of it. I'm all alone! Alone! The last, the last of? Thirteen! I count the lifeless bodies as they lie in horrible positions.

Crashing a bomb into their little dug-out, in case of treachery, I destroyed the neatness of this little home. The packs, black square packs, ranged along a wooden shelf. Packs that would never more be worn, and helmets! Yes, all in a row.

Prussian helmets … but I was sick, at heart. My best friend had gone … gone forever.

A strange desire arose in me. I bend down and take the bayonet from that rifle of that German, the 'hun' that killed Lieutenant Wedgwood. Pulling out a handkerchief, I tie that bayonet alongside my own scabbard, as a souvenir, to this day a memento treasured by me.

ALL ALONE!

I am all alone. I start up. The Battalion have passed far ahead of me. I must catch up. They have stormed the second line. I can hear the hoarse yells, the clash of steel, and the bombs!

THROUGH HIS BRAIN

At the double I start out. Around large shell holes, through rusty wire, I rush forward.

'ON GUARD'

It looms up: a big figure in field grey, from a hole in the ground. A Prussian? A fine figure of a man. Rifle and bayonet – at the 'on guard' – an unspoken challenge to duel? I'm in no mood for a bayonet fight just then. I flashed my rifle up – to send a bullet crashing through his brain.

Another Hun had crossed the 'great divide'.

IN NO MOOD FOR A BAYNET FIGHT JUST THEN I FIRED AND A BIG PRUSSIAN "WENT WEST"

JIM. MAULTSAID

INSTINCT, if you will, compelled me to glance behind. To my astonishment, a very young German soldier (a mere boy) was in the very act of sending a bullet through my back. As I turned he lost his nerve and ran, throwing the rifle down. I fired, a snap shot, got him! Hell! He crumpled up. Some poor mother's son. War! Hellish war!

Breathless, I take up with my chums again, just in time to storm the third enemy trench – our objective! 'Come on boys!' Captain Willis leads the way. We swarm out after him. A rushing, tearing bunch of war-stained youths. Withering fire greets us, but over the ground, and on! On! Stout resistance here. We are in! Amongst them. Hell for leather now. Swaying bodies, locked in a deadly hand-to-hand struggle. Groans! Curses! The death rattle! All sense of right and wrong forgotten – the desire to kill, kill, and kill! Unable to stop myself, I half hesitate, then jump, down into a party of three enemy soldiers. Too close for the use of any arms, I flashed out a right-handed blow – and dropped a German for the count. That blow almost smashed my wrist. My two feet had crashed right on the chest of one man – his chest was crushed in but I kept my balance. A rifle butt rises, and falls – a sickening thud – and the third man slithers down; his brains are scattered over the rifle of a member of my section.

AMIDST all the carnage of this bloody battlefield there was one incident that made me laugh – a grim laugh perhaps? But I could not resist. Collecting some thirty-five prisoners, I ordered them to empty their pockets – this was speedily done. All the stuff was thrown in a heap: watches, chains, money, pocket books, etc., etc. I was after revolvers, but none

appeared. Satisfied, I now wanted them into some kind of order before letting them loose into the direction of our lines. I gave the command to form up. They did not of course understand, and they were shaking with fright. Suddenly a little fat man (I took him to be a sergeant) rushed out, saluted me in a very brisk style, then proceeded to put up the prisoners in formation, in his own way. Oh my! How he manhandled them. He kicked them. Then biffed them. He pulled their ears – in fact everything but bite. He practically set each one in his place, then signalled to me that the job was finished and, by heavens it was! Well finished too!

I had to laugh outright. War was forgotten for the moment. One old fellow started to cry, the tears streamed down, down a fine black beard. He opened his breast pocket and waved aloft a large-sized photograph. I looked at it. A large family group. My heart was touched. Would I spare him? Shure! I nod approval. He put out his arms to kiss me. Nothing doing, thank you!

Poor "Kid Lewiss".

Another man offered me his helmet, the big German eagle all shining on the front of it, in the sun, if I would spare his life. Poor fellow, I did not want his helmet, or his life. He kept both.

THE END OF KID LEWIS

Shouting to Kid Lewis, I ordered him to escort his lot back to our lines. The poor 'Kid' started off like a shepherd after the sheep (much to his disgust), and the little fellow was never heard off again. I sent him on this errand to get out of the fighting; he should never have been in it, but he never came back. He was numbered among that awful band 'missing believed killed'. Poor Kid Lewis. A great little hero.

DOWN the line came the order 'dig in' We commence. Entrenching spades are hastily put together – we dig like fury. Thirty yards or so in front of the old German third line. We did not make any effort to reverse this trench, as had been the custom in earlier battles of the war, and a d★★★ good job too! Shells screeched overhead. Shrapnel burst above us. Big black coal-boxes came over with a noise like an express train. The German artillery had that line of theirs measured to the very foot, but the British troops were missing!

The sun shines down, hot, hot and intense. Our throats parch. Water! Water! was the cry. Most of mine went to the wounded. We toiled, we cursed, and we sweated. 'Sergeant! Give me a drink, for God's sake,' was the cry from a chum. I hold the bottle to his mouth – his chest is a real mass of blood and … a gurgle … he 'passes on'. Sick at heart, I turn away.

WONDERFUL 107 BRIGADE

A RIPPLE of excitement travels down the line. What is it? Here comes 107 Brigade!

They were to pass through us and take the fourth and the fifth lines. Steady as a rock, they streamed forward. Moved down in dozens, and scores, they are not to be denied.

Pride of Regiment wells up in my breast. 'The Rifles' – good old Irish Rifles. They are beside us! Great fellows, these men from Sandy Row, Shankhill Road, Dee Street, and the Antrim Road – magnificent troops.

THROUGH THE FIFTH LINE

'Come on boys! Join in,' shouts a grim-faced sergeant.

We throw down the little spades, grasp our bags of bombs, and rifles. Like the sea, we surge forward, storming the fourth line, and the fifth, and far beyond.

Through! Yes! Through all the enemy defences of Thiepval Ridge – over and out – far beyond our objectives laid down, out into the green slopes looking down on Grandcourt. What a victory! Glorious! And grand! But our numbers were getting thin.

Here in my humble opinion the battle was lost. No reserves! Our work well and truly done, but the advantage not taken – to land a smashing victory for British arms.

I had a feeling now that there was something wrong. Where was the 32nd Division on our right? Not a sign of them! And the 29th on our left? No sign either. Hell! We were 'in the air'. Looking away down across the swamp opposite Beaumont Hamel, I could see our troops advancing again and again across no man's land like little ants – to perish before the German front-line wire entanglements. Held here, as in a vice.

We were in for it now.

Prisoners had streamed past us, hands held high, and running hard, but parties of enemy troops were still holding out all around us. They fought to the last, and died for their beloved Fatherland like true soldiers.

BACK! BACK!

Gradually we fall back. Shot down from front, and both flanks, we were being wiped out. Surrounded on three sides it was now a hopeless position for us.
BLOWN up several times I escaped death times out of number. The shells rain down. It's desperate now! Midday passes.

HOW THE 107ᴛʜ & 108ᴛʜ BRIGADE

A temporary bridge over the Somme.

CROSSED THE ANCRE
—— TO THE ATTACK

THIEPVAL WOOD

SCORES —— AYE HUNDREDS OF THESE BRAVE BOYS PERISHED IN THAT AWFUL WOOD

JIM. MAULTSAID

HERE THEY COME!

Here they come! Coming in their thousands. Jerry throws his reserve battalions against us. Field-grey hordes swarm up – we put up a withering fire. They melt away. Come again. More! More! More! My rifle goes red hot. Our guns from the woods in Aveluy and round about Martinsart blow big gaps in the advancing masses. The French 75s crash shells into them at a terrific rate, but little parties drift through.

A GASP ... DOWN...

Yard by yard we retire. Every inch of the ground sold at its fullest price. We leave the old pals who slip down with a gasp, blood squirting or gushing out from a terrible wound. What could we do? Some crawled after us. Others lay still forever. Swish! A hissing sound, a rushing of wind. The trunk of a big burly Inniskilling beside me walks back several yards, his head blown off. I gasp! I shudder!

EDDIE SAVAGE – MY OLD PAL

I tumble into a communication trench. A body lies on its back staring up at the sky. Lifeless eyes. Peaceful, and restful. I look again.

It's poor Eddie Savage, my old platoon chum. Those big eyes haunt me yet. I take his hand. Poor old Eddie. My throat is raw. I fold his hands on his breast, and leave him as he had fallen.

FIGHTING – BACKWARDS

Back! Back! Still pressed by an overwhelming force, we retrace our steps still facing the enemy. Where in the name of God is our supporting division – the 49th? So far not a single supporting unit has reached us.

All mixed up. A bunch of Skins here, several Irish Fusiliers there, then Riflemen. Battalions had become platoons. I took any lot that came within my grasp. I had Donegal men, Tyrone men, Derry men and Belfast men at various times under my command.

Officers were scarce. They had been wiped out in dozens.

BITTER DISAPPOINTMENT MEN

Surrender! Not us! We would die fighting – and we did.

Did the enemy get a single prisoner from the Ulster division – a fit man? I don't think he did. Such was the spirit of the boys. But we were bitter now, disappointed men: we fought bitterly. We sold our lives dearly. The afternoon wears on. Tired out, body and soul, but our spirit still aflame, the battle sways to and fro. Ground lost, is retaken – and lost again.

SERGEANT MAULTSAID!

The Huns have commenced a new mode of attack. Bombing squads are creeping in from all angles; in, from, and down old communication trenches, from shell holes, they are hurling hand grenades at us.

'Sergeant Maultsaid!' Lieutenant Monard yells an order at me. 'Gather a bombing party – and attack down here', pointing to a battered deep piece of trench. Hastily I take five or six men, most of them from the Skins and lead that 'suicide squad' to certain death. Bombs were anything but plentiful, but orders were orders, and we were all there to carry them out.

TREACHERY! REVENGE!

Round a traverse we go.

Crack! Crack! Crack! I spring back! The door of a large dug-out stands before me. Shooting from a dug-out? 'Watch the other door boys,' I yell, and slam a Mills bomb into the blackness of the stairway.

A muffled explosion. Cries and moans float up. I slash another bomb in; their cries were as those demented. Commotion further back. Out rush several German soldiers. Bayonets flash in the sunlight. No mercy for them. Our boys are mad – mad with anger.

'Steady my lads! Steady!' I tried to restrain them.

WONDERFUL DUG-OUTS

Hands held high, over a dozen swarm out. Scared to death. We spare them with great reluctance. Down the stairs I go, a bomb held ready, and yell 'Surrender! Kamerad'. All was darkness. My eyes peer down. The moaning was pitiful to hear. I feel sad, sad. Nothing to fear, I go down, step by step. Can I ever forget that scene of carnage? A wonderful dug-out. Stocks of all kinds stacked up, foodstuffs, and ammunition, deep in the bowels of the earth. No wonder they could stand up to our bombardment. Out and out German thoroughness, in every line of that dug-out.

BOMBS – FROM THE DEAD

Pathetic eyes, appealing looks from the German wounded. I soften a little, but it's hard to forget that volley from this very place – and time is now precious. Pushing a box of mineral waters within reach of two badly shattered lads, I climb back up the stairs to emerge, just in time. My men were bombing hard, trying to stem a Hun advance down the communication trench. I take command again, and lend a hand. Bombs are running out. Mine are all gone. I scrounge around and pick up a few from a dead comrade. Bang! Bang! Not five yards away. Those German bombers are getting our range.

Swish! I duck. Bang! Right on the top of the parapet. Closer still! All our bombs are gone – we can do no more. 'Get back boys,' I order, and cover the retreat with my rifle.

COVERING – MY SQUAD.

Crouching back behind the side of battered traverse, I wait, ready to shoot. Round comes an arm, then part of a body. I shoot! Crack! Crack! The result was a shower of stick grenades. They fall short, but very close. I retire hastily. It's too hot here, and that bombing squad are strong in numbers and ammunition. Fearing a rush over the top and a speedy end I beat it back, back to my own companions.

I SLAM A MILLS BOMB INTO THE BLACKNESS OF THE STAIRWAY. THE .... CRIES AND MOANS FLOAT UP.

REVENGE.

COME ON! COME ON! YOU B—

PLOP! HIS BODY CRASHES DOWN BESIDE ME POOR FELLOW...... ALL HIS EARTHLY TROUBLES ARE OVER.

RAPID FIRE

I had fallen into the hands of my own platoon commander once more, Lieutenant Monard, and I was delighted. 'Here they are again boys!' The news brought to life the weary troops – troops who were dropping with sheer fatigue, and utter weariness, to a sense of danger. Jerry had launched another strong counter-attack.

We scramble up the battered sides of the trench, to get a field of fire. Coming! Yes! By heavens, they are – in full force. 'Let them have it boys. Rapid fire!' Lieutenant Monard coolly stands up and shoots as fast as he can, setting a great example.

SIGHTS – AT 100

Our rifles blaze. Two hundred yards, one hundred and fifty, down to one hundred. Crack! Crack! Crack! Still those grey forms come on, almost shoulder to shoulder. Holes are blown in their ranks. We can still shoot. Our numbers are small but we put up some deadly work with our 'best friend', the rifle. They falter. We raise hoarse cheers. Lieutenant Monard shouts 'Charge!' and we follow him up and over the rough shell-pocked ground. Seventy … fifty … twenty yards – all is a mad whirlwind. Bombs! Bayonets! Boots! A swelter of blood, and death in every shape and form.

Curses – and – cries … I hardly know what I'm doing. Oh! God, for a drink of water. My tongue hangs out. Water … water.

OFFICERS ARE SCARCE: JUST A HANDFUL LEFT

Figures turn and scurry back! We smash the counter-attack, by sheer bluff. How many of that tired band crawl back I cannot tell; but a mere handful I do know fell or collapsed – back into that old battered German trench. We were almost 'done up'.

EVENING FALLS

Evening comes. This awful hellish shellfire keeps on. We do not now even make any attempt to dodge the shells. Body and soul are almost at breaking point, but the spirit to fight to the end is still strong. No surrender!

Gathered in small groups. Officers are almost a rarity – they have nearly all gone. We bunched together for companionship and moral support.

All hope of support from the rear has now gone. We dimly realise that our hours are numbered. Surrounded on three sides by an enemy far superior in numbers, it sinks into our bemused brains that it's all up.

COME ON! COME ON! YOU ********!

'Christ Sergeant! This is a mess!' I look at the speaker. He wears the badges of the Irish Fusiliers and is quite young. 'By heavens you are right chum – tis' a hell of a mess.' Jumping up, he laughs – a horrible laugh – and waves his arms at the German position then shouts, 'Come on! Come on! You b******!' Plop! His body crashes down beside me, all in a tangle. Poor fellow. All his earthly troubles are over.

SEVERAL OF MY PALS DISAPPEAR

Whizz! – Bang! Bang! Bang!

A bright red flame! Smoke and dust choke us. The ground quivers – and several of my pals of a few minutes ago have … disappeared. My heart sinks low. I crawl on my stomach across a reeking shell hole to haul in a body that lies half out, and half in, over the brim. The movement brings a shower of bombs. I see at a glance that my companion is beyond all aid.

They are bombing! Bombing! And bombing! Gradually, one by one, these deadly missiles catch us, and our numbers grow fewer and fewer. Platoons are now mere skeletons of half a dozen men.

UP AND DOWN

… he bobs, that big black-bearded German bomber, throwing them like a machine. A brave man, no doubt about it! A wonderful thrower.

Captain Renwick, our machine gunner, who has long since lost all his gunners, guns and ammunition, clambers right up – stands straight bolt upright – and takes deadly aim. Crack! He runs the risk of a speedy death, but fear is unknown to him. No good! Again that black beard jumps up; I can see him distinctly for a brief moment. Whizz – crash! A bomb hurtles through the air. Captain Renwick grows desperate. Regardless of all danger, he stands up and shoots a full magazine at the barricade behind which lurks that deadly thrower. What a pest! We have not a single bomb to throw back. It's horrible. It's hopeless. It's desperate now. That blasted Hun has created havoc in our ranks; our party grows smaller. Captain Renwick decides we must rush the barricade, over the top, on each side, and close in to wipe this nest out of existence – or they will wipe us out.

OVER-AND-ONWARD! SCRAMBLE. RUSH. CHECKING THE GERMAN BOMBERS.

WHERE IS THE 49th ?

Some twenty men take part: Skins, Rifles and Fusiliers. Over and onward! Scramble! Rush!

An encircling movement, that yielded little or no reward, except a little peace. The big black-bearded fellow had gone, scuttled back down the communication trench. We drew a blank. Did he return? If he did, I did not see him again, but his companions did, and worried us, took a mighty toll of us, harried, and fretted us. Oh, for a supply of Mills bombs again. Where in the name of the saints has our supposed supporting division got to? Could the 49th not face the German fire? Or did they face it – and all perish?

THE DAY wears done. The sun goes down … down, on as bloody a battlefield as this old world of ours has ever witnessed. The slopes of Thiepval run red with the blood of Ulstermen. Dead in heaps. Dying in hundreds! God above us! This is glorious war! Huddled together – surrounded – the end is near.

DAMN – THE FEAR!

Surrender? Damn the fear! I'll die here first. Shadows are creeping in … in towards us. 'For the honour and glory of the old country boys, stand fast!' I entreat, and I implore. Coloured lights soar up. Shells crash down. The earth trembles, and those shadows creep closer, closer. Rifle flashes stab the half-darkness. Friend and foe are now almost unrecognisable. All is utter confusion. Every man for himself. We are fighting, back to back, a lost hope! Bullets rip, and rip around us. The gun flashes of the Germans are not thirty yards away. We yielded ground as little parties are simply wiped away – clean away. Survivors crawl back, turn round, fight, then retreat again, but still facing their front, dying in their tracks!

CRASH!

CRASH! I'm done! Like a thousand-ton hammer, it strikes me. The rifle drops from my grasp. I spin round – and round. All the world is going round in circles. I'm clubbed from the back with the butt end of a rifle? No! Anger and annoyance struggle for mastery.

Then blood, blood, blood everywhere, all over me. I can feel it. I sink down. It rushes in a hot quick gush from my mouth, it streams over my breast, and the back of my neck. In the name of God where am I hit? I tried to lift my right arm up to my head. It refused to act. My right arm gone? Will I never be able to box again? Or sketch? Hell! I'm finished.

Rough hands grasp me. I groan, they turn me over on my face, cut the equipment straps away, cut the khaki jacket clear, and pour a bottle of iodine into the open wound. I quiver – the pain is terrific.

GREATER LOVE HATH

'Now Sergeant! You'll be as right as rain.' In the glare of the gun flashes I could see two young boys from a sister rifle battalion bending over me. Cutting one of my puttees clean off, between them they bound my wound as best they could.

I have wondered a thousand times since that fatal night who they were. Did they survive? How I should love to meet those heroic boys once again. One binds me, the other takes up his rifle, and shoots, all to save an unknown sergeant! My strength is running out. I'm smothered in red hot blood.

I GAZE … AND GAZE

Around me, over me, surges the hand-to-hand battle. A handful of Irish lads, fighting to the end. 'Come on, Sergeant! Get out of it.' My friends lift me boldly up, push me over the back of the trench and shout 'Crawl back, you can do it.' I tried to stand up. My legs wobble, and down I slide. No strength left! I'll crawl! What a journey! Can I ever forget? With all its tortures, all its miseries, and the heartrending sights. I crawled over??? Never! Never! Never! Like a red-hot poker searing the flesh, the memory of that journey is imprinted on my brain.

HE SPEAKS? WATER! WATER!

C–R–A–S–H!   I'm thrown high into the air, and fall with a sickening thud on my useless right arm. The pain! It's terrible. My eyes close. I give up the struggle; the struggle to live, the will to survive is gone. Let me rest, and die. What's that moaning at my side? I take a slight interest. A weak voice whispers 'Water, water'. A voice with the noise of death in it. Where does it come from? Beside me, set up against the side of the trench, is a German. I lie and gaze, and gaze closer. Was it a ghost? A trunk of a man, both legs gone, one arm gone, and the top of his head blown off: yet he speaks; I want to live again! I work my hand, my left hand, slowly round to my water bottle – I raise myself up, and place the nozzle of the bottle in the poor creature's mouth, a bottle that contained not a drop of any liquid. His teeth snapped through the top of the mouthpiece, like a rat-trap, and the trunk slides down. The spirit has gone. God above me! This is WAR! Even as I write a lump rises up in my throat, and I've held that bottle again, in my dreams.

STOP! I'M GOING TO SHOOT

MAD! ... RAVING MAD! ...

Torn hands covered with blood, I struggle back, yard by yard. Every foot I move is now a torture.

Forms are crouching in corners, in shell holes. Indistinct huddled forms. What are they? 'Stop!' The cold muzzle of a revolver is pressed into my forehead. 'Stop! I'm going to shoot you!' An English officer going to shoot me? 'What for,' I gasp out in astonishment. 'You're a deserter!' 'What the hell are you talking about, I cry out? You are mad! Raving mad – and if you are so fond of shooting, for God's sake get away up there and help the Irish boys to do a bit.' My blood boils. He stoops down and gazes into my blood-soaked face. 'Sorry Sergeant!' he whispers hoarsely. I pull myself upright by the aid of some empty ammunition boxes. I sway, my head reels, the blood again gushes from me, all over me.

'Give me your revolver and I'll take your men up there – where they should be.' Poor fellows, they are badly led. The officer is ashamed, he is a bundle of nerves, he has lost most of his reason. 'Yes! Straight ahead,' he orders his platoon out. They file past me, and fade out into the inferno! My strength gives out, the strain has been far beyond it. I reel, and fall down, down, down – HELL.

I'm being dragged along now. Rough kind hands grip me by the back of the coat collar and haul me forward. He stumbles, and falls forward. I'm sliding forward – and down too.

The sunken road. Yes! Yes! And that road was littered with dead and dying. The most awful cries rent the night air. It was a … shambles, it was HELL – with the lid off; it was! But why describe it? Crash! Crash! Crash!

The Germans have laid down a barrage of terrific shellfire. They smash – and crash amongst all this.

My unknown helper has lost me – or has he, poor soul, 'paid the price'? On! On! A wild desire to escape takes possession of my soul. I'm afraid! Yes! I know real fear now. I want to live … I want to live! How I ever got through that sheet of red fire, our own cruel barbed wire, remains, to me, a blank.

I'm falling again! My fall is broken. Something beneath me squirms. It's soft. Oh, horrible, horrible! Can I ever get out? Our own front line again, near the top of Elgin Avenue, and I have fallen among stacks of dead men, stacks of them.

Dimly, a well-known voice penetrates to my brain. It's a voice I know. It entreats. It empowers. It threatens. Yes! I have it now.

Captain and Adjutant Mulholland.

He is urging the disorganised, and the demoralised, troops of the 49th Division out to help us – us, his beloved boys. Those poor mishandled troops would have been a thousand times better off out in no man's land. Huddled and hunched in this wood of death, they were simply slaughtered. Someone had blundered, and blundered badly. These were our supports, our relieving forces, and the enemy guns were killing them in hundreds.

SERGEANT TOM MURPHY.

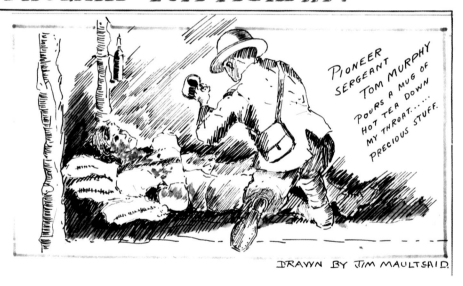

PIONEER SERGEANT TOM MURPHY POURS A MUG OF HOT TEA DOWN MY THROAT...... PRECIOUS STUFF.

DRAWN BY JIM MAULTSAID.

SLOWLY through the wood, I drag my weary body. I'm almost done now. The loss of blood has been draining the life from my frame.

I'LL NEVER FORGET

'Sergeant Maultsaid? By all that's above me – it's you!' Pioneer Sergeant Tom Murphy bends down and lifts me into a little shelter at the edge of the wood. Hot tea is poured down my throat. Another mug of that precious stuff is again forced into me, and new life runs through my veins, the first drink since 6.30 in the morning.

Sergeant Tommy Murphy, I'll never forget you – and your mug of tea.

... FADES AWAY ...

I can walk now. I thought I could. I must have slumped down somewhere about Aveluy Wood, or the road beside it. I come to, to find myself supported by two Inniskilling boys, one on each side. Then one of them staggers and falls down – he can go no further. His chum pulls him to the ditch by the side of the road. I cannot help. I am told to 'go ahead myself'.

On my hands and knees I move forward, up the road to Martinsart. Martinsart! At last! At last! In the hands of the Red Cross. Lifted up and placed on a stretcher, carried in to a dressing room, I remember the prick of a sharp needle – an injection? And everything fades away … away … away.

Bump! Bump! Bump! Oh Lord, the pain is terrible. That right side and shoulder of mine! I tried to turn over, but couldn't. A groan escapes me. My eyes take in the new, and strange, surroundings. Our motor Red Cross van!

Field dressing stations!

Red Cross vans!

Dressing stations again!

All pass in a hazy recollection across my memory. Where I was, who I was, I hardly knew! A train journey! Yes! I can remember opening my eyes and blinking. Was it an angel? No! Not an angel from up above, but an earthly one alright.

WHITE SHEETS AND PILLOWS

'Are you comfortable Sergeant?' 'Yes! Sister, I'm fine.' 'Good! Now just take this – and go to sleep.' I'm happy once again! Happy and content.

WAR-BITTEN TROOPS

The base hospital at Étaples – or was it Boulogne? I don't know. It was a Canadian hospital, I know that. They were so kind. Clean white sheets, white pillows – all was so bright – and good, for poor hard, war-bitten soldiers. All was so strange.

CLOTHES – BOOTS – AND ALL

They carry me – two men attendants – and slide me into a bath, clothes, boots and all, to soften the hard caked blood and strip my body of all the rough army shirt, coat and pants. Off comes my puttee bandage, from the wound. I grind my teeth with pain – pain that sends me swooning away.

... HOME ... HOME

I wake up, also swathed in bandages. A ticket is attached to my shirt front. I'm for Blighty. Home … home.

Down the gangway into a big hospital ship – the stretcher is placed in a kind of bunk arrangement. The boat is moving out, and heading for England. I cannot as yet believe that all!

I hear the waves wash past the side of the ship. The engines throb, throb, and throb. I close my eyes and sleep.

HOME! HOME!

DOVER! ENGLAND!

A TICKET IS ATTACHED TO MY SHIRT COLLAR FOR ENGLAND!

DOWN THE GANGWAY ON A STRETCHER.

PICTURES FROM THE STORY ON PREVIOUS PAGES.

JIM. MAULTSAID.

I CAN HEAR THE WAVES WASH PAST . . . .

. . . . I CLOSE MY EYES AND SLEEP.

HOMEWARD BOUND.

JIM. MAULTSAID.

DOVER! ENGLAND!

DOVER! England! And home!

Red Cross trains await us. We are carried ashore and placed tenderly in a corridor compartment. The last stage almost of our journey from the battlefield. It's London! Hurrah for London, but, no, we switch off somewhere and I land in Melton and Woodbridge in Suffolk.

TENDERNESS AND CARE

A big private house stands in large grounds. It's a VAD[2] establishment. A beautiful home, a wonderful place. All the sisters are volunteers, like ourselves. Care is lavished on us. Tenderness and care. Hands were not too experienced perhaps, but it was 'heaven' to me.

My wound was from a bullet that had entered below the collar bone high up on the right front side of the breast and smashed its way right through my body to emerge right in the centre of the shoulder blade at the back, leaving a large, ugly, ragged hole.

ROONEY? RODGERS? KELLY?

I lie for weeks and weeks on my face, as I could not bear the pain of lying on my back, or side. Weeks of agony, and torture! Sleepless nights – restless days. I lie and think – and think of that awful summer's day, 1 July 1916, on the slopes of Thiepval.

How had my chums fared? Had my platoon officer, Lieutenant Monard, come through? Sergeant Kelly? Quartermaster Ernie Powell? Joe Johnston? Tommy Rooney? Rodgers? Kelly? Alfie Mulholland? Tom Worthley? Doe Mitchell? And the rest? All the others. Of course, I knew dozens who had 'gone forevermore'. Had I not seen them fall with my own eyes?

PROUD OF THEM ALL

But we had made a mighty name for ourselves. The fame of the 36th (Ulster) Division had flashed from France to all the ends of the earth. The war correspondents sang our praises: 'one of the greatest feats of the Great War'; I was proud of those chums of mine – proud of my own Regiment, The Rifles, proud of the Skins, and the Irish Fusiliers. MAGNIFICENT ULSTER BOYS!

---

2. Voluntary Aid Detachment. Created in 1909 from the Red Cross and the Order of St John, there were some 74,000 VAD members by 1914, two-thirds of whom were females.

MY THOUGHTS GO – BACK – BACK

THE SUICIDE SQUAD.

By the talk amongst the boys this was a job that was not fancied a great deal, but the bombing squads did not worry much; we were happy-go-lucky bunches of lads, handling our homemade 'death dealers' in a carefree way, yet not careless; it was just experience and practice. We lost very heavily on 1 July – but carried out all orders in such a manner that our help and assistance was in a way the secret of such a wonderful attack. We took the storm troops out of numerous difficult positions. Here's to the boys that were nicknamed the 'suicide squad'.

GRENADIERS.

THE FAMOUS № 14 PLATOON

NUMBERS ARE AGAINST BOTH PICTURES ON THESE PAGES. MOST OF THESE BOYS ARE MENTIONED IN MY STORIES.

1 LIEUT WRIGHT.	11. CAPT. WILLIS.	21. McBRIDE. "FATHER"	31. RAINEY. SAM.
2 LIEUT MONARD.	12. McFADZEAN. V.C	22. SCOTT. BILLY.	32. HARDING. R.
3. MAULTSAID. JIM	13. MAGEE. JIM.	23. CLARKE. DONALD.	33. BOWMAN.
4. KELLY. NED.	14. KELLY. NED.	24. JOHNSTON. JOE.	34. McCOMISH. S.
5. BLACK. {STANLEY. PORKEY.	15. "DONAGHADEE".	25. LONGMORE. B.	35. MORGAN. A
6. BLACK. ROBERT STANLEY.	16. CALDWELL. E.	26. HOLDING. STANLEY.	36. BOWDEN. W.
7. ROONEY. TOMMY.	17. RICKERBY. JACK.	27. KENNING. JOHN.	37. McDOWELL. L.
8. McCLAY. W .	18. MONTGOMERY. G.	28. DAGLEISH.	38.
9. GORDON.	19. TOWE. JOHN	29. McCOUBERY. JACK.	39.
10. ROGERS.	20. JACKSON. JIM.	30. HAMILTON. "SCOTTY."	40.

No. 14 PLATOON.

SOFT THE NIGHT

As we pass along on our way to the line, a faint moon shedding its watery rays down upon us, we pass a little French graveyard. Just behind the reserve trenches where we laid you, old pal, a few short weeks ago. The little cross shines up: your form, your very self, comes back to us.

HAZARDS MANY

I can feel you, see you, hear you now as we soldiered down the years – facing our troubles side by side. Through the mud of the Somme, through the rain and the slush, our bodies starved and cold, but somehow never losing heart – just living in hope of better days, and the end of it all.

THE CAUSE IS WORTHY

Your heart was a staunch one, old pal. Sure to win in the end, if we can stick it – and by the holy smoke we can do that. Just wait until we get the guns, and the shells, then heaven help Jerry. No more sitting and waiting – no, my boy, we move forward to victory.

A RIFLE LESS

You will not take your place tonight on the fire-step, no share of a bacon rasher for you in the cold dreary dawn after 'stand-to'; God, but it's cold tonight – ah! you still march with us, down the old French road, to the firing line, old pal of mine!

TO THE HOUR AHEAD

Mind the sump hole. Splash! Splash! Steady in front. Why are the boys so quiet tonight? Are their thoughts racing backwards – back to our last term in these very trenches – when YOU, dear friend, walked amongst us all?

WILLIAM MCFADZEAN

WINS THE VICTORIA CROSS

By an old comrade.

GREATER LOVE HATH—

14 18278 Private WILLIAM FREDERICK M'FADZEAN, 14th Batt. Royal Irish Rifles (Ulster Division).

For most conspicuous bravery near Thiepval Wood, on 1st July, 1916. While in a concentration trench, and opening a box of bombs for distribution prior to an attack, the box slipped down into the trench, which was crowded with men, and two of the safety pins fell out. Private M'Fadzean, instantly realising the danger to his comrades, with heroic courage threw himself on the top of the bombs. The bombs exploded, blowing him to pieces, but only one other man was injured. He well knew his danger, being himself a bomber, but without a moment's hesitation he gave his life for his comrades.

Private M'Fadzean was a son of Mr. William M'Fadzean, Rubicon, Cregagh, Belfast, and was born in Lurgan, in 1895. He was on the staff of Messrs. Spence, Bryson & Co., Belfast, before joining the colours.

PACKED IN THE ASSEMBLY TRENCH

EACH BOMB WAS FINALLY EXAMINED AND PINS SLACKENED

THE BOX CONTAINING 12 MILLS BOMB'S SLIPS DOWN — DOWN INTO THE NARROW TRENCH.

SKETCHES BY — JIM MAULTSAID

THREW HIMSELF DOWN ON TOP OF THE BOX KNOWING HIS DANGER.

PROUD OF HIM – ONE OF US

Proud of him? Proud beyond expression of our boy. A big genial fellow, free as the wind itself. A bomber of the very first order, and he died as a real bomber should, amongst his deadly toys.

As a brother of the 'suicide squad' I was indeed elated to learn that Willie had gained the greatest honour any soldier could gain, but sad to think that such a young life had paid the price to save his chums! Willie boy, your name shall live amongst us until, one by one, we go to the same resting place as you.

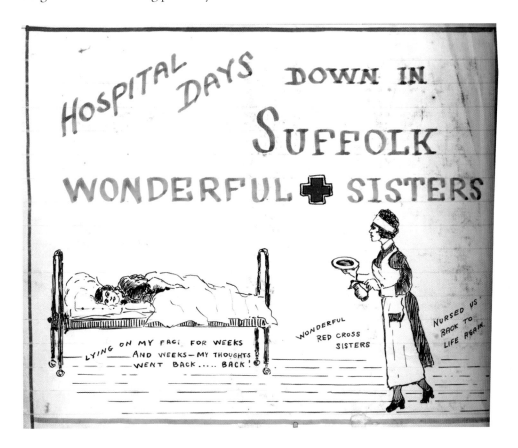

DOWN IN SUFFOLK

A fine big mansion, lovely grounds a bunch of Red Cross VAD sisters who could not have been surpassed for kindness – what more could a war-broken Tommy ask? No wonder I rapidly got well – under the care of these wonderful girls. Weeks of agony passed away, as in a dream, then a joy day as I was allowed to sit up and take notice. It was a case of strawberries and cream – is it all true – or am I to wake up and find myself in a filthy dug-out once more?

I sit and look at the clean linen sheets. I gaze at the pot of real English flowers from the gardens outside. I can't understand it all yet, after that 'Hell' over there. 'Are you comfortable Sergeant?' God bless her – she's a darling!

FIVE SONS OF ERIN

I whisper, 'She's Irish!' Daughter of an Irish lieutenant general, born in India, and full of Irish lore. More Irish than I am – yet she has never been to the Emerald Isle! 'Is the grass as green as they say it is – over there Sergeant Jim?' 'Yes! Sister it's as green – as green almost – as you.' 'None of your blarney my lad – or you'll get no strawberries.'

IRISH AND PROUD

We lie in a big room, five of us – all Irish. Munster, Leinster, Connaught, Tyrone and Down. Put here by order, all in one place. If we want to fight, we can have it out amongst ourselves. Fight! Ye Gods, there is not an inch of fight left in the five of us. This daughter of Erin has been specially detailed to watch over us – she's a tomboy.

SO HAPPY

My face has been washed at least half a dozen times today, bandages – miles of them – wound around me, and I feel like an Egyptian mummy – but so happy. Here comes the doctor. Bustle, scurry and hustle. 'Easier today, Sergeant?' 'Yes, Doctor, a lot.' A kindly old American doctor looks at my wound – and passes on.

OUR FIRST NIGHT – OUT –

WHEN THE LIGHTS WENT UP – ALL THAT WAS LEFT OF OUR PARTY – WAS – YOURS TRULY – AND THE SISTER IN CHARGE.

I DASH OUT AND MAKE FOR THE LOCAL PUB

FOUND THEM ALL THERE SWINGING THE LEAD

FALL IN!

I REPORT TO THE SISTER PARTY, – "ALL PRESENT"

–ILLUSTRATED BY JIM MAULTSAID.

WHAT a treat was promised us. Pictures! We had not witnessed real pictures for over a year. After months of pain and suffering, you can well imagine our delight when news came through that we were all to go and see the local cinema programme.

The big night arrived and we duly took our reserved places in a very dark and small picture house. There were about twenty of us and we were under the care of a young sister, 'Yours truly' in charge. Very good. All went well until half-time.

I wondered why the troops were so quiet. Yet I thought I heard strange shuffling and movements.

MISSING!!!!

The lights go up! God bless my soul – not a single man in blue[3] was in the place. Where in the name of heavens had they got to? The little sister was in a state. Excitement was at fever pitch. Uproar and confusion. She was in for the sack now! I smiled and told her to keep cool. A brainwave flashed through my brainbox. Stay here sister and leave this business to me.

TELLING THE TALE

I knew that the village of Melton and Woodbridge possessed at least a couple of public houses, and that this was the first night out since coming back from France. What price a drink of real old English beer? My spirits dropped low as I drew a blank at No. 1 call – no luck! Not a single 'swatty' there. At the double I made for the other bright spot. In I dashed. Yes, they were all inside, telling the tale.

'Fall In! Back to the picture house. Quick March!'

THE WILD IRISH (BY ONE OF THEM)

MISUNDERSTOOD

THE idea some of the English people had about Irishmen was – well, we were just wild, wild men. I was surprised and amused when matron gave orders to have us (all the Irish boys) placed in a room by ourselves, so that, if we wanted to fight, we could have it out just between ourselves. Fight! Not a bit of it – we had had enough of that.

SOFT SOAP

Our special sister was Irish too – or had Irish blood in her veins – and she could fairly handle us – no mistake about it. Soft soap and soft words. We would have done any mortal thing for her. Just a lot of big overgrown boys in her hands, those men from Munster and Leinster. Rich in humour as per usual, their deep brogue amused the sister. She would imitate them. Sure and begorrah … .

---

3. Soldiers undergoing hospital treatment wore blue uniforms.

IRISH TEA

Midnight strikes! A soft step sounds on the stairs. I lie awake. Sleep is hard to find. The door is now open and a shadowy figure steals in. Whispered words. The little sister is going from bed to bed. My turn comes. 'Would you like a drink of hot milk, Sergeant? And stuff with the kick in it – or hot tea?' The kick was not 'official', of course – and my milk was 'milk' only. 'By my stars that is great stuff, Sergeant!' 'What a great war this is.' 'Shure, an I'll go out again – get wounded and come right back to this very place once more.' These were the expressions from the other four beds, so the hot tea was 'real good stuff'.

'Now keep quiet or I'll stop your rations,' whispered our angel as she bade us all 'Good night and God bless you all'. Good night! Good night! A home from home. 'Worth fighting for, the likes of her,' says Munster as he drowsily slips down and passes into the land of dreams, war and pain all forgotten!

READ THE STORY

I fall for Eve

ON our way to the a party on a hot summer's day – yours truly in charge – we rested by the roadside. A smart pony and trap drew up. The driver, a smart young lady, speaks to me. I knew her as a visitor to our hospital. Would I like to go for a drive? The boys said yes for me. How the devil could I go and leave the troops? 'Go on, Sergeant! I'll look after the boys,' a young lance-corporal speaks up. I fell to the charms of Eve, and hopped aboard the trap. The sun shines down. Glorious day in the country – time passes. Tea and hot scones at a farmhouse. Tis good to be alive. The evening creeps on – we turn the smart pony homeward. I wonder how the boys have fared and have qualms on my own account. This is desertion, and I'm liable for court martial; still no, I'm not in the Army now, or think so anyhow. So run my innermost thoughts.

HELL OF A STEW ...

Round the corner of the drive and the tree-lined avenue to our home of rest. Say girlie! – how quiet it is. Not a sinner about. Ye gods! They have not returned yet. I slip in and make a survey. Not back yet. Dashing down the avenue I meet them – all in fours – just as tight as they could be – but quiet. I discover they have never been to the party.

God bless me – what would I do now? 'Don't worry, Sergeant, it's all right.' Hell, I was in the stew now! A troubled night for me. Commotion and flutterings at the front door early next morning – the lady who had the tea all spread out for us is looking for the Matron. I have already opened my heart to our Irish angel and she flies out to square the indignant lady at the door. A BARGAIN IS STRUCK. WE HAVE TO RETURN TOMORROW AND EAT ALL THE GOOD THINGS. WE GO! YES! AND OUR MATRON NEVER KNEW.

IT SEEMED A LONG TIME ago. In fact, it seemed hundreds of years ago since I had set eyes on the auld shores of Belfast Lough. Long before the steamer had reached Irish waters I was up on deck straining my eyes through the morning mist on the lookout for a sight of the Emerald Isle, 'that island of delight and dreams'. Oh, how the boys used to rave and sing about our little bit of home – and here it was now almost at hand. The sun breaks through as we gather (a bunch of war-weary, hard-bitten Irish boys) and a cheer breaks out as the shores of Auld Ireland loom up: Blackhead! Donaghadee!

JOY AND GLADNESS

Hurrah! Hurrah! Excitement runs hot as we pass Whitehead, Bangor, Holywood and Carrickfergus. Then the great iron girders of Queen's Island and shadow skeleton boats glide past. The docks, the quay, then Belfast. Down the gangway we scramble and rush. Home! Home! Home! Wonderful home! I am dazed. Bewildered. Can it all be true? Or am I dreaming? Never did the city look so fair and sweet.

THE OLD LISBURN ROAD

I set out and walk all the way home. My arm still in a sling and bodily very weak, but I slowly walk along and drink in High Street, Donegall Place, the City Hall, Dublin Road, Shaftesbury Square, and the good old Lisburn Road. Good to be alive? You bet!

I stop at the top of Melrose Street and gaze down. Never did I expect to see it all again – then the last few yards are covered. I push open the gate of No. 44 – hesitate, then ring the bell.

Great joy! I'm amongst all my loved ones once more. Kindness is showered on me. It was great and glorious to have fought for them.

POSTED TO THE RESERVES

IN THE OULD COUNTY DOWN

THE end of all good things must come sometime and my ten days were now spent. I had orders to report to Newcastle, County Down, where our reserve battalion, the 19th Royal Irish Rifles were in training.

OLD PALS

What a meeting! It was 'Hello Jack!' 'Hello Jim!' etc., etc. Old pals, privates, corporals and sergeants – one after the other all the way. 'Glad to see you.' 'And you?' 'How goes it?' Handshakes and good-natured banter. All the returned wounded from the 14th and 15th Battalions were there, also a lot of young recruits and a cadet company of young officers in the making. What a mixture!

THE LAST IN THE LINE, D COMPANY

Medical inspection – posted to D Company once more (would I never get away from the last of the line?) – marked unfit for any duty. Here I was in a home of rest. What more could a returned warrior ask?

HAPPY – CARELESS – FREE

Back to tents and lazy days. The cool breezes from the Mourne Mountains swept down; the sea breezes put new life into our bodies. We slowly revived and took an interest once more in life. Happy, careless, carefree days were these. My wound slowly healed up – my arm gradually lost its sense of numbness, but the shoulder still pained me a great deal.

A WONDERFUL MO

One of the finest medical officers I ever met was in charge here. One of nature's gentlemen, he was kind to all the boys who had come back from the war. Unfortunately, I cannot for the life of me remember his name or I would set it down on record. Also, the good people of Newcastle? They tried their best to make us forget the past – with all its tragic background – and live for the future.

Captain Buchanan

WE boys who had returned from the war were called BEF men (British Expeditionary Force) and we were all kept in one company. So the brotherhood was strong. All of us were wounded, gassed or injured on active service in some way, and our captain was one of us – Captain Buchanan of the 15th Rifles. A stern just man, but a warm spot in his heart for 'his boys' had our skipper. Did we give much trouble? Not a lot. Any slight 'diversion' by us was glossed over. We were far too happy and contented now – sadder, but wiser, men than in 1914-15. War had chastened us all.

A RARE JOB

One of the rarest jobs that came my way during my Army career now fell to my lot. I was put in charge of the 'cripples' or bad cases. My work each morning was to take these men out for a march (it was a country stroll) after breakfast. We walked away from camp then picked a quiet spot, sat down by the roadside, and smoked.

Yarns were swapped and 'battle' tales were re-told. I heard the story of the 15th boys – how they had suffered and triumphed. We became fast friends. I was deeply interested in their history and to this day have many great chums from this grand sister Regiment. Great lads, these 15th men!

SINNED MY SOUL

Weekend leave to Belfast was frequent and I often sinned my very soul getting passes signed for the troops. I was out to let them get the best I could as I knew in my heart many of us would have to go back – back to that HELL in France and Belgium, and, in return, these boys never once let their little sergeant down. Heaven help the man who had done so – his pals would have murdered him, I do believe. But we stuck like glue to each other – we BEF men.

COLONEL WALLACE

ONE of the finest gentlemen it has ever been my pleasure to meet.

Commanding officer of the 19th (Reserve) Battalion Royal Irish Rifles, he was one of the finest gentlemen it was ever my pleasure to meet during the Great War 1914-19, kind-hearted to a degree unknown in my dealings with men and commanders; the men would have done anything for him.

THE SOUTH DOWNS

He was an old soldier of the Boer War and Indian warfare and commanded the South Down Militia with great distinction. Possessed of a fine voice, he sang and also composed a very popular song called *The South Down Militia*. Rendered by himself, this was one that always 'went over' with a great swing and the chorus taken up by the boys brought the house down.

GENEROUSITY

As a sportsman he excelled. He loved sports of all kind and took a deep interest in football, boxing, and field sports – in fact any sport. It was nothing for him to offer him £10 or £15 towards prize money for these events.

One dealing I had with him stands out in my memory. My papers had been sent out from France to the reserve battalion suggesting that, as I was no longer fit for active service, I should be put forward as a candidate for a commission in the Labour Corps and be of some better use than in the reserves. He sent for me and told me the proposition. It was a surprise I agreed. Later a hitch occurred. I was American born, and no foreigner was granted a commission in HM Army. 'Well!' I said, 'I have already fought and bled for the old country and if that is not good enough, I'm finished. No more France for me.' He laughed and said, 'Quite right, Maultsaid! We cannot send you back. Leave it all to me, and I did.' How he succeeded you will read later.

LANCE CORPORAL KEARNEY

A WONDERFUL BODYGUARD

TOUGH

Lance Corporal Kearney! What a fine old Irish name! Big and tough. A nose that had stopped something d★★★ hard many years ago. It was flattened out and bent sideways. Standing six feet or more, he was a hardy looking son of Ulster. A product of the 15th Rifles, somehow he took a fancy to me, always if possible doing the same duty as I was detailed for. I had now got to the stage where I was called on for Sergeant of the Picquet on pay nights (Fridays). This was a rough business sometimes as the boys 'hit up' the Newcastle pubs, having a few shillings to burn.

'PUB' DUTY

Closing time was at hand. Animated scenes in the pub. Loud talk. Some swearing and jostling – good-natured banter, and some not so good natured.

UP AGAINST IT

'Squad halt! Stand at ease! Easy!' I enter the 'den of booze'. Pushing my way to the counter, I smash my small cane on the marble-topped counter. 'Finish your drink boys and clear out! It is time you were going back to the barracks!' Silence. Then a half-drunken soldier makes his way over to me and leers into my face. 'What the h★★★ are you talking about?' A pin could have been heard dropping. It was indeed a critical position for me. I draw back. My left hand closes – I think like a flash. A left hook, and you'll go out – out to the world. Steady Jim! Your rank must be upheld.

ROUGH STUFF

Like a whirlwind he came. The 'drunk' was snatched up by the scruff of the neck and seat of trousers. Through the swing doors like a streak he was thrown: Lance Corporal Kearney to the rescue.

THE OLD GAME

BOMBING INSTRUCTOR AND RIGHT! RIGHT!

A NEW JOB – SPELLBOUND

'Sergeant Maultsaid will take charge of the recruits and bombing practice tomorrow.' So said the battalion orders. At it again! 'Gather round my lads and I'll tell you a story.' They sat spellbound as I went back over history: from the days that our troops made their own bombs from jam tins, bully-beef tins, etc., and how they made them. How they fought with them against Jerry's stick grenades. Then came our Mills bomb, our stick grenades, our shooting bombs from a rifle. All the rest of it. All the special virtues required from a 'bomber'. The sacrifice. The constant training. Demonstrations – with my left hand. How to throw – how to keep up with the supply of bombs. Then the story of my famous squad on that July day at Thiepval. How they fought! And Ned Kelly – the Army's best thrower.

THE STORY

Our VC bomber! Willie McFadzean. Eyes open in astonishment as I unfold the stirring days – days of struggle and strife. 'Now boys, let it all sink in. Just make up your minds to rise to the same standard of efficiency as these men I've told you about. You can all do it! And don't forget the honour of the old Regiment we are all so proud of! Dismiss!'

I WONDER

'Right! Right! Keep the distance. You broke your mother's heart, you want to break mine?' A new pastime for me. Squad drill! Raw levies. Clumsy as can be. I like their eagerness to try and do the right thing, and forgive their little faults. 'Shun! Trail arms! Quick March! Number Six, stop hopping about, let your feet down. Very good boys. Halt! Dis – miss!' A dash for the tents – and the cookhouse. Poor lads! I watch them … and wonder: what is the future to be for them?

SPORTS

I TRAIN IN SECRET

HEAVY BETTING I TAKE THE HUNDRED

SEVERAL of my brother NCOs hatched a plot, but did not tell me a word about it. A big sports day was ahead. It had never dawned on me that I could still do the hundred. In my heart I thought my running days were over. 'Jim! Will you train for the hundred yards?' a chum in Mess put the question to me. 'Sorry, I'm no use now,' was my reply. 'Ah! Come on now for the fun of it.' 'All right old man, I'll have a shot at this event.' Secret training was to be the order. Up the Mourne mountains we went – found a quiet spot of straight level surface – and commenced. A fortnight of this and I was feeling very good. Then the fun commenced. How, I don't know, but the betting began. I was at about 8 to 1. Bad! Indeed I was considered as an also ran. Pounds, shillings and pence were invested on me, by my NCO chums only. Our skipper, Captain Buchanan, offered to cover every pound won in prize money by his D Company – a fine offer.

ALL NEWCASTLE

The day arrives. All Newcastle and the surrounding country gather in. Sergeant Major Elphick has everything in apple-pie order. The band plays. Dozens of runners for the sprint. Some six or seven heats had been run off. I did not fear one of the winners – except Cadet Ballantyne (an old 14th man): he was 'class'.

Could I beat him? My heat is called – we line up. Crack! Off! I sail home an easy winner. Down goes my price. You could not get even money now. A dark horse!

UNSPOILT BY WAR

I rest on the grass. Exhausted. The old 'blowers' are not what they used to be. Thank the Lord the final in which I have to figure is down the programme. The cadets are all young fresh fellows, unsoiled by war, as yet, many of them.

The hundred. Final! A deep silence falls as we face the starter. I watch the muzzle of the starting pistol (an old trick of mine). Flash! Away we go, down the incline. I lead, no one in front. I know in my heart I'm the winner. Halfway. The crowd yell 'Come on Jim.' 'Come on Sergeant.' 'You win.' 'You win.' A deep breath. The final spurt. Arms out flung. A wave of pleasure runs through me as I breast the winning tape. THE WINNER. I'm caught up, shoulder high, and carried to the dressing tent. Good old D Company.

NOT TODAY MY SON

A race for NCOs only. I'm on the scratch mark: 220 yards this time. Comrade-in-arms Sergeant Major Ernest Powell is my hottest rival. We banter each other coming down the straight for home. Side-by-side. 'This is a gift for me, Jim,' pants out Ernie. 'Not today, my son,' says yours truly. I pull out, draw to the outside, pass several rivals, take the 'rails', and WIN, easy. More £.s.d for me.

£ 16.0.0 IN ONE DAY

The relay race is always a much sought after inter-company event. The BEF men were keen to win, just to show the younger fry how to do it. I was one of the big four. Truth to tell, I was about 'done up', but turned out, and ran a good race to put our lot in front of the cadets – and took the laurels for the old firm.

A GLORIOUS DAY

A glorious day but a far better morning followed. Captain Buchanan kept his word and paid out. My share was somewhere around £9.0.0 from him. £16.0.0 for a day's sport. A great life this – in the Reserves.

CERTIFICATE FOR BRAVERY

IT had been whispered to me that I was recommended for the DCM[4] – whispers only. Would I get it? Of course I was pleased to hear it – what soldier was not? – but was wise enough to put little faith in these little bits of gossip. I would wait and see – like Asquith!

IN ORDERS

To cut a long story short, there was no DCM for Sergeant Maultsaid, but orders came through that some dozen or so NCOs and men were awarded a special certificate by our 36th (Ulster) Division for acts of bravery and leadership. My name appeared in Orders. Well, in a way this was even better than a medal. I would have it in black and white and could always look back and 'romance' again on that black tragic day, on the slopes of Thiepval, when we fought … .

FOR THE 1 JULY BATTLES

The Commanding Officer planned a big day, as some six or seven of the boys that had won these illuminated certificates were in his reserve battalion at the time.

DOWN FROM THE MOUNTAINS

The band played. Troops were formed in to a square all facing inward. Standing apart inside the square we were lined up in order of rank. The officers formed a section on their own.

'Battalion S'hun!' Regimental Sergeant Major Elphick's voice booms out. We all spring to attention. The General Officer Commanding in Ulster steps forward, Captain Buchanan a few paces in his rear with the scrolls of honour in his hand.

Names are called. Each man steps forward, salutes, receives his 'reward' and a handshake, salutes, and smartly steps back.

My turn comes. I received mine. I feel pleased. It's all over now, almost. A speech of praise from the GOC to the troops. The troops are asked for three hearty cheers. The echo comes down from the Mourne Mountains. 'Dis – miss!'

---

4. The Distinguished Conduct Medal, then second only to the Victoria Cross as a gallantry decoration for other ranks in the Army. It has since been replaced by the Conspicuous Gallantry Cross, for all ranks in all three services.

BUT – IMPORTANT

HE ambled around – and his job was picking up scraps of paper, rubbish and camp litter, placing this in a bag carried for the purpose. Badly wounded, this was a real 'soft' job for him, and he knew it. Hardly bending his back even, he just stuck the long-nailed pointed stick through the offending paper. Job! Then into the bag. Slow? As slow as a snail. No rush, and no excitement. He just moved on at his own pace – and all the 'red caps'[5] in the Army would not have speeded him even one-mile-per-hour quicker.

The boys often kidded him that he was 'working his ticket'. In fact, he suffered a lot from the chaff and banter of his chums, but seldom replied. He just grinned.

Something brewing!

Down the lines he came one fine afternoon, all smiles, beaming – indeed radiant. Dressed up in spick and span togs – puttees and all complete (he had never been known to wear putties since joining the reserve Battalion) – and such a 'knowing' look on his face. Something was in the air without a doubt. What was it?

Before he reached the bottom of the lines, a crowd of almost fifty interested spectators (including myself) were following him. Something drew us on – dramatic events were in the air.

---

5. Red cap, in this instance, is a reference to a staff officer. At this time, all officers on the staff, irrespective of rank, wore red cap-bands and had red tabs on their uniform collars. The soubriquet 'red cap' later came to mean a military policeman as the Corps of Military Police wore caps with a red cover.

ONE OF THE TROOPS

Slowly he turned, faced us, and, putting his hand into a breast pocket, brought out a large-sized envelope. This he tore open, and extracted a blue form. Holding it above his head, he blandly said, 'You all took me for a d★★★ Fool, but h★★★ r ★★★★ the one of yez could have picked up a paper like this from the parade ground – like me.'

IT WAS HIS DISCHARGE – HIS TICKET.

A travelling medical board struck Newcastle like a thunderbolt from the sky. Dozens of us were marked for active service again: A .1, according to our reports.

Lord bless me – fit again? I could not even lift my right arm as high as my shoulder. Could not lift a rifle, and the wound was not even healed up. Sore and soft to touch – and here I was to go back once more to France. God! This was some position to be in. But what could I do? Orders were orders. I was for it, fit or not. I prayed for strength to carry on. I was both weak and ill.

FALL IN THE DRAFT

Not an hour's leave to say goodbye to our loved ones? Yes! We got forty-eight hours' leave as a great concession – and said 'Farewell' once more. Back to Newcastle.

'Draft will parade in full marching order at 10.00am and will proceed to … under the command of … for Foreign Service.' This is an extract from Battalion Orders.

I STARE STRAIGHT IN FRONT

'Fall in the draft!' How my pack strap cut into my shoulder. 'S'hun! Medical Officer will now inspect the draft.' We stare straight in front of us. Slowly he comes down the line, a list of names in typewritten foolscap paper in his hand. He is before me. 'Sergeant Maultsaid!' 'Yes Sir!' A look at his list. He turns to Regimental Sergeant Major Elphick, and says, 'Why is this man on the draft, RSM?' 'I don't know, Sir.' 'Sergeant Maultsaid, fall out!' A curt order from the MO. I WAS SAVED FROM WAR.

SHORTLY after this a bunch of us were transferred to that godforsaken camp opposite Newcastle – Ballykinlar camp, land's end as it was called, and well named. Winter days. Cold nights, no outlet, no social life. It was like a prisoner-of-war camp. You made your own fun – football, sports, concerts, and all the rest. Dreary days. I almost wished I had not been taken off the draft. The only relief was a pass now and again home to Belfast. If I sinned my soul in Newcastle telling lies trying to 'wangle' passes for the boys, I doubled my misdeeds here. I missed the orderly room several times by inches – all for the boys. What a life. But some funny incidents cropped up.

Read on, and laugh.

WANTED, A HUNDRED MEN

CHURCH parade in the Army was a grim affair. One fine Sunday morning I was in a h★★★ of a fix. The parade 'roster' called for two hundred men for church parade. This was impossible as my full parade only mustered one hundred men. Where had my 'beauties' gone? And where the devil was I to get another hundred troops? Truth to tell I had let far too many of them away on leave, and now I was for it – yes, good and plenty. A brainwave flashed through my thinking box.

Could I bluff the orderly officer? I knew he was shortsighted, but a blind man could almost see that one hundred was not two hundred. Still, I had them on parade early and gave them a short sharp lecture.

DO YOU FOLLOW ME?

Something like this. 'Listen boys – I'm in a h★★★ of a stew. I'm one hundred men short. Get me?' They did! 'Don't show any surprise at the orders I will give. When I say "march" you march no matter a d★★★ what religion you are. Then sort yourselves out later. Do you follow me?' Broad smiles! Yes! Sergeant 'Boko Compree' – bad French for full understanding.

THE PHANTOM ARMY

Church parade S'hun! All present and correct Sir. Yes! This is the R.C squad. They number off – one hundred strong. He inspects them – is satisfied – and gives me the order to 'move off.'

'RC party! Form fours! Right! Right wheel.' Off they go, as I yell 'Quick march!'

Now I had to give them a chance to mix themselves up a bit and make up a different formation and frontage, so I held him in chat for several minutes. 'Now Sergeant, I want

the Presbyterians and any others.' 'Very good, Sir, follow me.' We make our way round several large huts – and arrived on the parade ground allocated to the PEs and the A. others.

'Squad S'hun! Number. One hundred strong.'

He steps forward to inspect them. Lord! My heart was thumping now. Will he, will he know any of them? I sweat. Cold sweat trickles down my spine as he peers at them minutely. Is my 'big bluff' to be exposed? 'Move off Sergeant.' I could have jumped for joy. I almost choked, my words of command seemed unreal to me. Saved! Saved! Saved! Out of sight, those wonderful troops 'sorted themselves out' and saved me from the Orderly Room.

I REPRESENT THE RIFLES

SERGEANT MAULTSAID 'will proceed to Chelsea Barracks, London, tomorrow morning – on a course. He will represent the Royal Irish Rifles.' I was not at all displeased at this turn of events as life in the reserves depot was dreary. No need to describe the journey to London; it was a case of darkened portholes and windows in the railway trains all 'blacked out', in case of enemy aircraft.

What a gathering!

What a gathering of the clans! Every regiment in the Army was represented, plus all our colonial troops. Never did I see such a varied collection of men and uniforms.

A BAD FALL FOR THE NCOs

My spirit rebels

What a shock we got first morning! Remember that at the 'school' were NCOs (nothing lower than three stripes) and the big Guards' sergeant pops his head through our door at 5.00am on a cold winter's morning bellowing, 'Up! You lazy b★★★★★★. Get your brushes, mops and the buckets of cold water down below – and every man take a section of the cement stairs – and scrub thoroughly for CO's inspection at 6.00am.' we gasp! The swearing was awful.

There was nothing for it but to start. I kept quiet – and carried out my job as best I could, but my spirit rebelled and I formed an instantaneous dislike for the Coldstream Guards – in fact the whole d★★★ Guards Brigade. This dislike I never lost, and never will. But you should have heard the Aussies and the Canadian boys. I thought there was going to be an open rebellion. Wiser heads prevailed.

On parade, washed and shaved at 7.00am. For what? Can you believe it

To learn the GOOSE STEP!

ALL IRISH FALL IN! Time 7.00am. St Patrick's Day in the morning! 'Parade S'hun! All Irish men – on the word of command – will take two paces forward,' and 99 per cent take those two paces. The CO gasped. So did I. Never did I dream that so many of my brothers in arms were Irish. The big burly sergeant major almost collapsed. But what could he do? Irish? Yes! Every d★★★ one of them, or so they said, and you cannot dispute it when a man claims the 'ould Green country' as his own. The officers were in a fix. Hasty confabs – and a quick decision by the CO.

'Well boys! Seeing you all claim St Patrick, there is nothing for it but to give you the day off! Dis – miss.' A smart right turn, salute. A wild war whoop – and St Patrick's Day was ours, free and do as you like, get as full as you like, and, and – but 12.00 midnight must see us all indoors. Midnight was a long way off.

No Redcap could lay a finger on an Irishman – on this one day out of the three hundred and sixty five days in the year. Hurrah! Hurrah!

I'M A SERGEANT IN THE RIFLES

Rolling home – Rolling home – blind drunk. Yes! Almost every mother's son got 'blotto'. Piccadilly, The Strand, Knightsbridge, had all their quota of 'drunks'. They were carried in, rolled in, brought in – in taxis, dragged in, in all shapes and condition. Did London ever see such drunks? I took a great interest in it all – and I enjoyed it, as the 'booze' had no charms for me. It was great steam. The Sergeant of the Guard stopped me at 11.50pm and said I was drunk. He ordered me to stand to attention when speaking to a Sergeant in the Guards. I told him to go to hell – I was a Sergeant in the Royal Irish Rifles.

A NEW experience for me. Never before had I been in the Zep raid. The planes were not uncommon bugbears to the troops, but big Zeps were certainly out of the ordinary to us.

A sudden darkening of the few darkened lights. All is darkness. Crowds rush past – what's wrong? I flatten out against a shop doorway and wait on events. Boom! Boom! Boom! Distant gunfire. Searchlights stab the blackness overhead. I don't like this business at all. Screeching, terrified women dragging children after them – aye – and strong husky fellows pushing them out of the way. A mad rushing mob, hell for leather, and the survival of the fittest. So this was a Zep raid?

I was disgusted at the animal behaviour of the men. Just wild animals – no thought for women or children here. I move on, groping my way yard by yard along the shop fronts of The Strand. Boom! Ploop! – Crash! By God, they are coming close. Bang! Bang! Big shells bursting in the heavens. Ploop! Ploop! My heart sinks; what an awful feeling.

The battle front was bad, but this – and we below? Helpless, and hopeless. God, it was awful. Never did I want to be in a Zep raid again. A terrific explosion shakes the very street, startling in its very nearness and unexpectedness, like the roar of a thousand howitzers. Plooooop. Crash! Are they after the War Office? And the Houses of Parliament? I crouch down, cover my head with both arms – and pray to God in heaven. A mighty explosion, flames. Flares light up the horizon beyond the top of the buildings. The drone of the engines I can now plainly hear: Zur! Zur! Zur! Something compelled me to look skywards, and there it is, a big long silver cigar-shaped object: a Zep! My first view and, I trust to God, my last.

LIFE! HECTIC LIFE

PICCADILLY IN WAR TIME?

Swirling! Hectic! Seething! Troops from all the far-flung battle fronts. White, yellow, black, all colours, all shades. The tower of Babel all over again. East and West. North and South. Young soldiers. Old soldiers. War-weary soldiers. WAACs.[6] VADs. Airmen – Tank Corps – kilts. Slouch hats. Pill-boxes. Tall hats, black-evening-suited gentlemen, and the young women – and the old ones too. Bad women from all the countries in Europe. Paris, Brussels, Russia, Japan, China – all the world over. Here in London town. How they haunted the bright lights – and polluted the boys in uniform. Stop to gaze at some window display – and you found a painted face, or two, at your elbow. 'Good night! Darling,' or 'How are you, sweetie?' Poor things! Hardly two words of English. They were, more often than not, 'foreign ladies'.

Up and down! Down and up Piccadilly, they paraded. Looking for pigeons to pluck – and I'm sorry to say many's a one was snarled. Life! Hectic, mad and swirling life. I stand in gaze, and watch it slowly ebb past, parade … parade … parade.

AN AWFUL SIGHT

Crash! Smash! Glass slashes all around me. A young girl staggers out on the pavement – half of her head split away, blood spurting from her, and collapses. I turn sick at the sight, hardened veteran though I am to the sight of blood. The public house door swings back. A small crowd collects. Whistles blow. A taxi swirls up, and she is lifted and thrown inside. She's young, but will never erase that awful scar from her countenance. Poor girl. I shudder, and move off.

Sickened as I never have been before, war days in London! Life! Tragic life!

---

6. Women's Auxiliary Army Corps, the predecessor of the Auxiliary Territorial Service of the Second World War and the later Women's Royal Army Corps.

We goose-stepped. We drilled, and we goose-stepped. Such useless stuff. How in the name of Mike would we win the war by this 'dope'. I was fed up. Parade! March! Parade! March! Were the authorities mad? What, or who, was responsible for this? Some b★★★★★ old dugout of a general who wanted to keep himself in a cushy job? Never did I have such senseless, useless instruction. Discipline! Discipline! H★★★ It was rubbish: 7.00am until 4.30pm, day in day out. The Guards? The Lord help them – if this is what they sent the recruits to France stuffed with. I could have drawn up a plan of drill and physical exercise far in advance of myself, something instructive and useful for foreign service.

WHAT A NIGHT

Dramatic orders were issued one fine morning to the effect that all the Irish troops were to be sent back to their various regiments at once. Passes were issued – we were hustled out of the barracks at top speed. What's wrong in Ireland? No one knew, and to this day I've never yet found out. They knew nothing about all the imaginary 'scare' at home. 'Wind up' for d★★★ all, as usual.

PRAYED – AS ONLY AN IRISHMAN CAN

I will never forget my trip across the Irish Sea on this voyage. It was the worst crossing I ever struck. Picture a dark evil-smelling hold down among the cargo, hatches battened down over the heads of the troops and the ship plunging, rocking, swaying over, up, under. Seasick, green-faced, khaki-clad figures all lying in a heap. Sprawled out dead to the world. Groans, moans, curses. I spent the entire night holding on for dear life to an upright iron post. At the peak of the storm an Irish cattle drover produced his beads and prayed as only a good Irishman, and Catholic, can pray. Safely into Holyhead. Cheers!

CAMBRIDGE

A BEAUTIFUL SPOT

TWO MORE RUNNING TRACK EFFORTS BEFORE I GO – AND THE RESULT

Colonel Wallace sent for me. He did not lose any time getting to business. 'There is word from the War Office, Sergeant Maultsaid. You are to report on [--------] at Cambridge and go through your course of cadet training for a commission, and feel yourself highly honoured, my friend, as you are not a British subject. Yet you're going to get a commission in His Majesty's forces. This is rare indeed. Good luck Maultsaid.' We shake hands and I thank him for all his good work on my behalf. A new life opens up for me. Several days' leave. I return, pack my kit, say farewell – but I'm held up for several weeks longer for some unknown reason and during this spell of idleness take part in two running track events, meeting my match in both. Still I was quite pleased as I had only been beaten by inches and the prizes were good. For all that, my heart yearned for my old-time form and speed and I felt confident that these events would have been mine without a doubt. The relay race was for the Championship of Ulster. So we did not do at all badly, this old reserve Battalion of ours, and we were all crocks too! Anyhow the trophy came to our own Regiment. My prize, a beautiful clasp knife, was handed over to Regimental Sergeant Major Lowry – to keep a longstanding promise. He was delighted with the gift and keepsake.

CADET WARD

FROM HUDDERSFIELD

HE was a rare turn – this man from Huddersfield. All our billet were Irish, except our chum Ward, and we got along in fine style. Such a good sort himself, he and I struck up a rare friendship as we discovered that sketching was a hobby we both loved and, my word, he could do the black-and-white stuff in great style; a real artist. I was more than delighted to meet him, and he was amused at my style. We simply fell into each other's arms, so to speak.

MY BLOOD RAN COLD

I had arrived at Cambridge. We all lost our stripes the first day. I now was Cadet Maultsaid, one of the common herd again, and was going to be drilled all over again. One – one – two. Left turn – by numbers. My blood ran cold. Still it had to be done.

Cadet Ward, poor soul, was at his time well into his forties and had never been in the Army before, much less France. I was of great help to him in many little ways and put him wise on shortcuts, all learned from bitter experience, and he appreciated all. As a matter of fact I was astonished to learn that not 5 per cent of the men on this course had ever heard a shot fired in anger, and yet these men were going to the officers! Of course, a big percentage were unfit for active service, their destination being the Labour Corps.

OUR MAGAZINE

WONDERFUL TALENT

MY LIFE'S AMBITION
Never was I so happy

It was not long until my abilities as a black-and-white artist were discovered. We had a magazine of our own and the talent was more than plentiful. Indeed it was simply there in all shapes and forms. Writers by the yard. Artists, pen and brush, abounded, and men who could produce a stage play in half an hour or so. It was wonderful! From all walks of life, they could have run a full-blown newspaper or posh magazine without the slightest trouble. You will agree with me when you turn the pages and see for yourself a few samples of their work.

A finer lot of gentlemen I never met. Everyone was an expert in his own line, musketry, platoon drill, signalling, etc., etc.; of course they were picked for that purpose, yet never lost their human feelings and assisted us to meet and overcome the snags of everyday life in the Cadet Battalion. A helping hand at any time was, as a rule, always extended to us. Most of them had already served abroad.

OFFICERS' GROUP.

Capt. A. W. CLIFFORD. Lieut. N. L. ANDERSON. Capt. G. GRAY.

[Stearn & Sons.

Lieut. P. D. MANN, Lieut. D. N. BARBOUR, Lieut. H. V. DACOMBE, Lieut. R. G. KARN,
Lieut. S. G. K. RAPLEY.
Lieut. W. R. H. WRIGHT, Lieut. W. L. McNAIR, Lieut. G. MACFARLANE-GRIEVE, Lieut. C. L. FERGUSON,
Lieut. G. FLEMING-BROWN, Lieut. R. N. C. HUNT, Lieut. A. C. N. SPICER, Lieut. W. N. E. BRUCE,
Lieut. A. D. IRVIN.
Capt. J. H. WYLIE, Major J. V. BIBBY, D.S.O., Major G. A. BLACKBURN, Major S. C. MORGAN,
Lieut.-Col. H. A. CRADOCK, Major C. C. SHAW, Capt. C. M. LLOYD, Capt. A. A. H. CHARLES,
Capt. and Adjt. J. STUART.

G O C B

Sketches by Lieut. Maultsaid.

By LIEUT. MAULTSAID.

G.O.C.B. CHRONICLE.

A. G. REID, 17.10.17.

A. G. REID, 17.10.17.

FROM OUR BATTALION MAGAZINE

THE LOAFER.

1ST MONTH AT CAMBRIDGE
Oh! for those Glad Rags!

2ND MONTH
Oh! for the Sam Brown!

LATER, Somewhere in England
Oh! to be back at Cambridge

BY FRANK REYNOLDS.

A MIDSUMMER (Common) NIGHTMARE.

G.O.C.B. CHRONICLE.

Sunday on the River Cam

Doorway & Cloisters
Jesus Colleg Cambridge

GREAT
TALENT

In the Master's Garden. Christ's.

Bernard Braham. 1917

No. 1 COMPANY.
Capt. A. W. CLIFFORD (Hospital), Lieut. W. L. McNAIR, Lieut. H. V. DACOMBE and Lieut. D. N. BARBOUR.

No. 2 COMPANY.
Capt. C. M. LLOYD, Lieut. A. C. N. SPICER, Lieut. P. D. MANN and Lieut. N. L. ANDERSON.

No. 3 COMPANY.
Major C. C. SHAW, Capt. J. H. WYLIE, Lieut. G. FLEMING-BROWN and Lieut. W. N. E. BRUCE.

No. 4 COMPANY.
Major G. A. BLACKBURN, Lieut. A. D. IRVIN, Lieut. MACFARLANE-GRIEVE and Lieut. R. N. C. HUNT.

No. 5 COMPANY.
Major J. V. BIBBY, D.S.O., Capt. A. A. H. CHARLES, Capt. G. GRAY, Lieut. C. L. FERGUSON, Lieut. R. G. KARN. M.C., Lieut. W. R. H. WRIGHT and Lieut. H. G. DASHWOOD.

COLLEGE CRESTS

First Court. Christ's.

"MISSED AGAIN SARGINT"

ALL FROM THE MAGAZINE

"MISSED AGAIN SARGINT" SKETCHED BY — JIM. MAULTSAID.

G.O.C.B. CHRONICLE.

Our first efforts on the miniature range reminded me of the story concerning a recruit who persisted, when firing, in assuming the position Sam Weller took up when writing his famous valentine.

After a monotonous sequence of " misses," the Instructor was fed up. Throwing a spare round to the rookie, he said, " Here, lad, go behind there, and blow yer brains aht." Rookie went. Followed a loud report. Horrified Instructor rushed round to find the recruit with a smoking rifle, and a grin across his face. " Missed again, sargint," he calmly announced.

J.S.W.

FILL-UPS.

The Cadet to his Mother :
Roses are red,
Violets are blue :
Send me five quid
And I'll think of you.

The Mother's Reply :
Violets are blue,
Roses are pink ;
Enclosed is five quid,
" I don't think ! "

His neck in a muffler of dingy red,
A cap with a six-inch peak on his head.
He lounged in a suit of threadbare brown
At many street corners in London town.

In a curious lethargy there he saw
A thousand men passing him, four by four.
In the shouts of the people, the blast of a horn
Imagination was bred and born.

Imagination was born, and bred
As he bound himself to his country's cause.
Imagination was knocked on the head
When he found himself in a sergeant's claws.

The sergeant gripped him and held him tight,
Drilled him and harassed him day and night
Till imagination was well nigh dead—
Then " Put up a stripe, my lad," he said.

And imagination was born again,
And he saw in the hardship and stress and strain
A something to live for— to die for too
If the fates were agin' such a fellow as you.

His sloth slipped from him, his soul was free,
And life was the contest it ought to be.
And though Death find him, the loafer then
Will be found as a man in the world of men.

M.

OF AGE.

When I was but one year old,
With a placid stare I watched the sun
Turning the fields to cloth of gold :
And little I knew of Stevenson,
And little I heeded what I was told,
And little I cared for romance and fun,
For then I was only one.

And when I was one and ten,
I lived in a world of sword and gun,
A world transformed by the magical pen
Of Henty, and Weyman, and Stevenson :
Ah, wild and free was my fancy then,
And I thought there was naught but romance and fun,
For then I was ten and one.

But now I am one and twenty.
I know there is shadow as well as sun,
And now I read drill-books in place of Henty
(Though I love no less my Stevenson) :
And I know, though adventure comes in plenty,
That life is not all romance and fun,
For now I am twenty-one.

What do you think of all our great and wonderful talent? I'm sure you agree with me when I say we had them with talent for almost anything. Take Cadet Ward: here was an artist and writer rolled in one, and good at both. Then Cadet Reid: he was just fine on the black-and-white stuff. Cadet Braham's pictures of the college were works of art. Cadet Frank Reynolds was our star turn in the funny line; his expressions are a treat, and Cadet Howell in his skit (the white band) should surely make you laugh – it's true to life – and describes in sketch the life of a cadet from the first day until the final exam is over. The boys that went in for it the poetry line I cannot judge myself, so leave it to you.

Of sportsmen we had dozens: boxers, footballers, runners, cricketers, rowers, tennis, and all the rest. My only regret being that, during my term of these three months at Cambridge, we never had a sports meeting.

THE WHITE BAND

BY   BERNARD HOWELL

"**YOU** HAVE BEEN SELECTED "!—

"**YOU**"—

WHO HAD LONG ERE THIS GIVEN UP ALL THOUGHTS OF EVER BEING "SELECTED"—ARE TO REPORT YOURSELF TO THE O.C. OFFICER CADET BATTALION - CAMFORD, ON THE 19TH INST.

IT IS ONLY NOW THAT YOUR SUPERIOR OFFICERS REALISE YOUR STERLING QUALITIES AND INVALUABLE SERVICES AND HOW SORRY THEY ARE TO LOSE ONE OF THEIR "MOST PROMISING N.C.O's"

THE GATEWAY TO THE PROMISED LAND?

THE ARRIVAL

THE "PIP"!

THAT SINKING FEELING

WHAT IT FEELS LIKE THE FIRST DAY.

"ALL TO BE LEARNT BY HEART?"

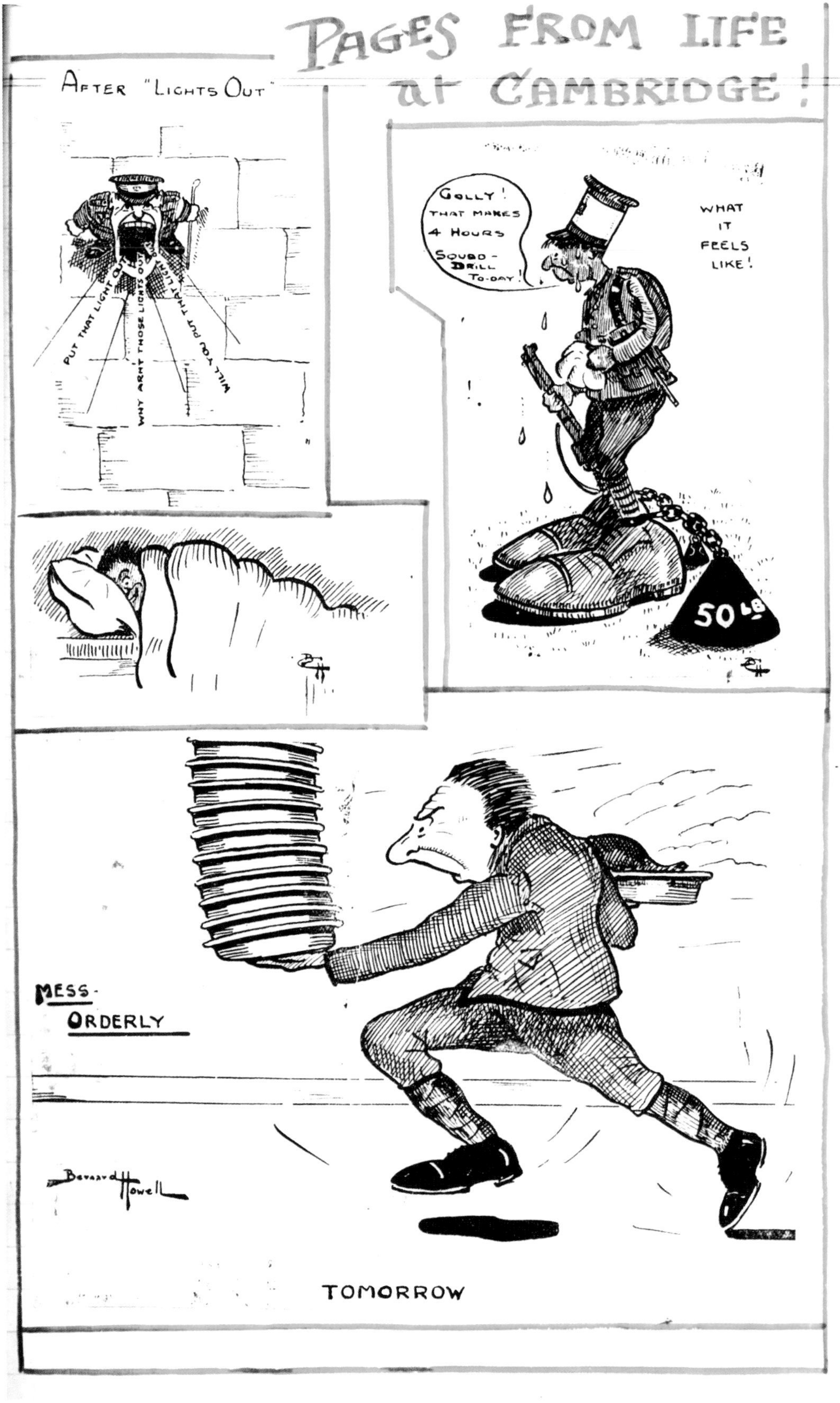
PAGES FROM LIFE at CAMBRIDGE!
AFTER "LIGHTS OUT"
PUT THAT LIGHT OUT
WHY ARN'T THOSE LIGHTS OUT
WILL YOU PUT THAT LIGHT OUT
GOLLY! THAT MAKES 4 HOURS SQUAD-DRILL TO-DAY!
WHAT IT FEELS LIKE!
50 LB
MESS-ORDERLY
Bernard Howell
TOMORROW

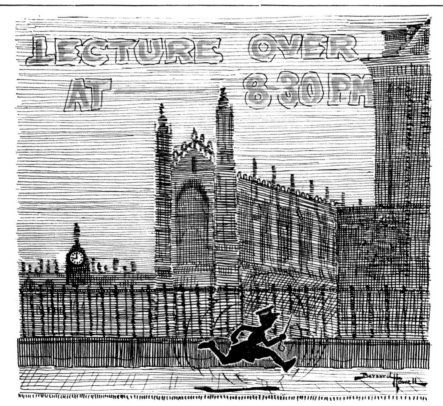

AFTER THE EVENING LECTURE YOU ARE AT LAST

FREE —— TILL NINE O'CLOCK

THE NIGHT BEFORE THE FINAL

LITTLE KILLERS

It certainly felt strange to me to sit and watch a demonstration of how to throw bombs, me that had been a bombing instructor in my heyday and had thrown these deadly little black missiles to kill! Kill! My God! And here we were being shown how to handle them. Just imagine my feelings! I felt a tinge of sadness too: to think of my wonderful bombing squad, and how we had been scattered to the four winds. Oh, for Ned Kelly, just to let them see a real thrower, or Eddie Caldwell: bombers all. Still, I had to sit and listen to a man who had never thrown a bomb in deadly earnest, or heard the swish of one coming over, or the awful feeling as you watched its flight in mid-air, and then ducked..

My mind was hundreds of miles from Cambridge, and my interest in the instructor was … nil. I could have taught him a few tricks myself. How startled they would have been had I taken a pin out, let the handle go and throw!

POOR FELLOWS

Bayonet practice! Let me say right here that on my first day at Cambridge on the medical exam I had been excused all physical exercise and the carrying of a rifle, so took no active part in these drills, just sat and watched.

A BOOT IN THE ...

A fine-looking fellow was the gym instructor. Heavy and well developed, but I think he could have been floored. What about some of my 'dirty tricks'? What price a fork for close quarters? Did he know that one? Would he gasp if I used the butt end of his rifle? Or a kick in the stomach? Yes, I could get him with all his poundage. But why romance; my days were over. The efforts of some of my brother cadets were pathetic – poor fellows. A good soldier from the 14th Royal Irish Rifles could have easily beaten six of them – and lost no sweat over the job. It was hard to watch. How they floundered about. Short-sighted – bad legs – bad chests – hardly a sound man amongst the lot. Easy for Jerry, this bunch. Poor fellows.

SANDBAG ART

Trench digging! I could stand it no longer, and butted in. Let me show you boys how to build. It was a wet day. We've dug deeply and the soil was good to work with. The platoon officer let me direct operations. I made them hustle – and the result was a very fine bay and traverse. So fine was the job my platoon commander went for the CO and he viewed our work. 'A great job, Sergeant. Sorry, I should have said Cadet.' (The three old stripes had gone.) Lieutenant Hunt was pleased. I had made my mark in his good graces. My platoon were simply delighted. We were set up as a model for the whole Battalion!

Visions of Beaumont-Hamel, Hamel, and Thiepval Wood – those trenches hewn out of chalk, and built with the tired weary bodies of countless Ulstermen, rose before me as I watched the trench slowly form and take shape.

BLACK OUTS

SKETCHES FROM ROUGH ORIGINALS

WONDERFUL CAMBRIDGE

OLD WORLD COLLEGES

THE OLD RUSTIC BRIDGES.

BEAUTIFUL OLD GATEWAYS.

LITTLE NARROW STREETS

OLD FASHIONED DWELLING HOUSES

THE RIVER CAM

WINDOWS HUNDREDS OF YEARS OLD

SKETCHES BY — JIM MAULTSAID — FROM ROUGH ORIGINALS

EVENING SHADOWS FALLING

ANCIENT DESIGNS

EARLY MORNING SCENE ON THE HEATH

EXPLORING CAMBRIDGE

HOW I love to explore. During our leisure hours I used to take solitary jaunts around the old world town. On these occasions I always carried my little sketching outfit and when I ran across an interesting view down it went for future reference and the joy of looking backwards. On the page opposite you can see some pictures drawn from rough original sketches. How those far off days come back again to me!

OLD WORLD STYLE

Little narrow streets, funny little houses, beautiful archways, old world fashions. And the colleges? Set amongst tall stately trees, green lawns and wonderful gardens. Oh, beautiful Cambridge! Flowing through the town was the River Cam. Winding in and out, flowing ever so slowly, was the river of dreams. An old punt drifts downstream. I wave a greeting to the occupants. War! War! It was far, far away. Cambridge the beautiful.

SPECIAL POSTER WORK

OH! SO HAPPY

AFTER my successful demonstration of 'Sandbag Art', my platoon officer asked me to do a large sized drawing so that he could lecture on the subject. Below you can see the original sketch from which I made the huge canvas drawing some 10 feet by 12 feet. Tins of coloured paint added the correct tint and, to say the least of it, my 'effects' were very real indeed. A very successful effort. For all I know, it may have been used long after I had passed out from the school. I was happy indeed at this work. Oh! So happy!

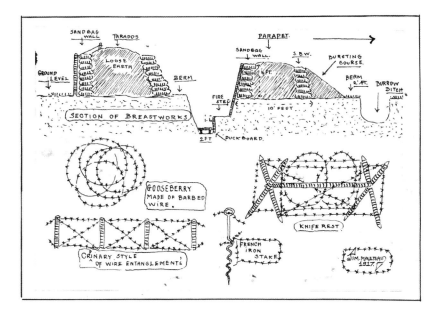

INDIA VS ENGLAND

AGITATORS

IN the college in which it was my privilege to be quartered (Magdalene) there was a section allotted to some Indian students (civilians) and these young men kept very much to themselves as a rule.

WE ARE CHALLENGED

They had practised carefully. Trained hard and studied our style of football. Challenge is issued. Would we play them a match? Would we what? Of course!

WELL BOOMED

Posters, handbills, and all the arts of advertising were used to boom the fixture: India Vs England.

Great football attraction! Roll up and see 'the match of a lifetime'! Comes the day. Crowds gathered. The pitch was wonderful. In fact it was a downright shame to play football on it. Lawn tennis courts had been swept away wholesale, and the sod was like a spring mattress – a sin indeed.

POOR INDIA

Off we go! I played in all departments, we simply walked through those coloured gents and taught them a lesson. I was the flying outside right and had the pleasure of banging home four goals. They introduced the rough stuff, got our backs up, and suffered. We were no lambs ourselves and gave more than we got – shoulder and boot in full measure. Nine good and true goals did we shoot past the men of colour. Poor India was indeed humiliated. That finished them.

'JERRY AGAIN'

AIR RAID! My dreams of blissful peace were rudely shattered. A dark night: the sky is ink black. All lights out! Air raid! Air raid! I could hardly believe it. My last raid in London came to mind and, truth to tell, I did not like the thoughts of having to go through the same again. What defence had we in these parts? Weak I'm sure. All blackness. Not a sound. We crowd out to the 'quad – and wait.

FROM THE SOUTH

Boom! Boom! Distant thunder rumble – rumble. Where is it? Voices are hushed. We whisper in undertones. Far away we could hear the dull booming, but could not place the direction. From the south the sky lights up, fades down again. Boom! B-o-o-m! London tonight again? It certainly looks like it. My heart goes out to those souls waiting for death from the clouds. My blood boils. Can we do nothing? The thunder seems to be moving around in half circle, away towards Oxford. Have they missed us?

I slip out from my chums, run through the college grounds, and stop at the banks of the Cam. Better out here, away from four walls, free and open – not like a rat in a trap. I feel much better now. Boom! Boom! Boom! I scanned the sky like a stargazer. It's not our turn tonight – and I'm not at all sorry. Dull rumblings gradually die away and cease altogether. The raid is over. 'All clear' sounds; I wend my way back.

DREAMING OF BOMBS

Two hours have passed away. I climb the dark old stairs, grope my way into my little cubicle, and wearily pull my greatcoat off to throw myself down and sleep, sleep, sleep, dreaming of bombs, shells, screamings, and horror-stricken women.

The home of horseracing lay some several miles from Cambridge. Some of the boys suggested a trip to Newmarket. Would I go? Yes, of course; I was anxious to see for myself this famous spot so I made one of the party that set out to tramp these miles. It was an adventure, and what young man can resist the lure of the unknown?

HAIL! NEWMARKET

Half holiday. Away we go. Fall in – and follow me. The mile posts pass one by one. We march on. Songs, and a musical instrument here and there, help us to forget ourselves; we swing merrily along. Glorious day, life was good and we were enjoying ourselves in this good old part of England. Hail Newmarket!

BEAUTIFUL FLOWERS

The Downs! Glorious Downs! Every yard of the course was traversed by us. The straight mile! The ditch! We examined them all. What glorious grandstands and beautiful flowers. But things looked a bit neglected, I thought. Of course, it was wartime and I suppose the gardeners were in K of K's army like us.

NO RACING TODAY

It was not race day, so we did not see any racing. It was in fact greatly restricted, this form of amusement, although carried on by the sanction of the powers that be, in a kind of a way.

HOT SCONES

The village is small, but neat and trim. We had a cup of tea, some hot scones and home-baked bread, (a treat for us these days) then our steps turned homewards. Lights out will soon be sounding. Roll call is almost at hand, we break into the double and arrive in the nick of time, just as the big iron gate is being swung outward to close up for the night. A happy day is ended. Good old Newmarket.

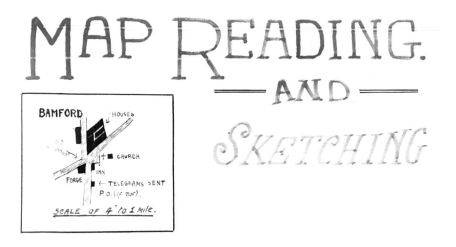

I was delighted with this part of our work as it gave me a great chance to use my sketching talent and naturally this pleased me. We spent all day at the business, taking observations, making rough calculations and pencil sketches. My book was then inked in at night and you can see the result on following pages. Lieutenant Grieves knew his job and took good care to make us do our work thoroughly. Some of the boys were inclined to regard this day as a kind of holiday, but he was having none of this and made them get down to business very soon, and jolly well right too. We covered many miles of open country around Cambridge during our 'map work', but it was great, healthy and, to me, great fun. A wonderful change from drill and barrack square stuff.

JIM MAULTSAID

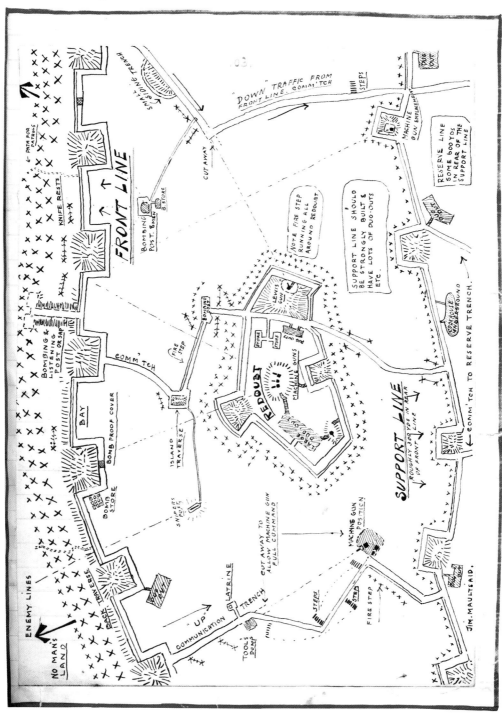

FRONT LINE

ENEMY LINES

NO MAN'S LAND

PATH FOR PATROLS

KNIFE RESTS

SMOKING TRENCH

"DOWN" TRAFFIC FROM FRONT LINE COMM'TCH

STEPS

DUG OUT

MACHINE GUN EMPLACEMENT

RESERVE LINE SOME 800 YDS IN REAR OF THE SUPPORT LINE

BOMBING POST & SMALL B. STORE

CUT AWAY

NOTE FIRE STEP RUNNING ALL AROUND REDOUBT

SUPPORT LINE SHOULD BE STRONGLY BUILT & HAVE LOTS OF DUG-OUTS ETC.

COMM'TCH TO RESERVE TRENCH.

BOMBING & LISTENING POST OR SAP

COMM'TCH

FIRE STEP

LEWIS GUN

BOMBING OUT

STORE

STORE

DUG OUT

SORTIE UNDERGROUND

DUG OUT

BAY

BOMB PROOF COVER

BOMB STORE

ISLAND TRAVERSE

SNIPERS POST

REDOUBT

MACHINE GUNS

SUPPORT LINE
ROUGHLY 300 YDS IN REAR OF FRONT LINE

COMM'TCH TO RESERVE TRENCH.

BACK TRAVERSE

LATRINE

"UP"

COMMUNICATION TRENCH

TOOLS DUMP

CUT AWAY TO ALLOW MACHINE GUN FULL COMMAND

MACHINE GUN POSITION

STEPS

FIRE STEP

JIM. MAULTSAID.

MAP READING

LECTURE ON MAP READING BY LIEUTENANT GRIEVES

Some of my sketches are labelled with Ulster names, as you can see. These are not imaginary drawings but I tacked on the Ulster titles, just for a joke. Villages, railways, cliffs, mountains, woods and of course rivers all came under our notice during our travels. The drawings are all from the military point of view and would not pass the civilian test I suppose, but then everything in our life was in the military strain. Cadet Ward, my old chum from Huddersfield, was simply great with his little black-and-white pictures and far outshone me in this line, but I had no ill will towards him. In fact I was delighted to see this all making such a good show as he was weak in the drill business and this gave him a chance to shine in this branch of our work.

A glorious day draws to a close and we return to college in good spirits and write up our records.

'FRENCH SYSTEMS'

DEMONSTRATION BY POSTER

MY fame as an artist, especially in regard to military stuff, was now more or less established in my own company and my platoon officer gave me every encouragement. He gave me a special commission to draw him a large-scale drawing of a series of 'French Systems' and all the special points to be carefully marked out. A large sheet of white canvas, some red, black, and blue paint, and a couple of hours on the work produced the picture on the previous page. First of all, I sketched the original in my book and planned it all from experience gained in France, true to life, so far as my own memory served me. You can now study the original drawings overleaf.

IN MY ELEMENT

The picture was a beauty and we had a lecture on the subject. I was called on several times to explain various points and their exact meaning. This, of course, was easy to me and I was quite pleased to do so. My travels in 1914-1915 stood me in good stead. One up for the old 14th Rifles?

The boys were all interested and, when the lecture was over, crowded around me for further information. Notebooks were freely used and sketches done from my work. I helped dozens to fill in the parts that baffled them – and it was surprising the questions I had to answer. Of course, a lot of my Cadet chums had had practically no experience of this subject, being straight from public schools and the OTC. I was out and out as happy as could be. Just my line. I had a little class of my own that night in my cubicle and explained all the knowledge I possessed to these willing listeners. Willing to learn, I was just as willing to teach them all I knew about this 'game' of WAR.

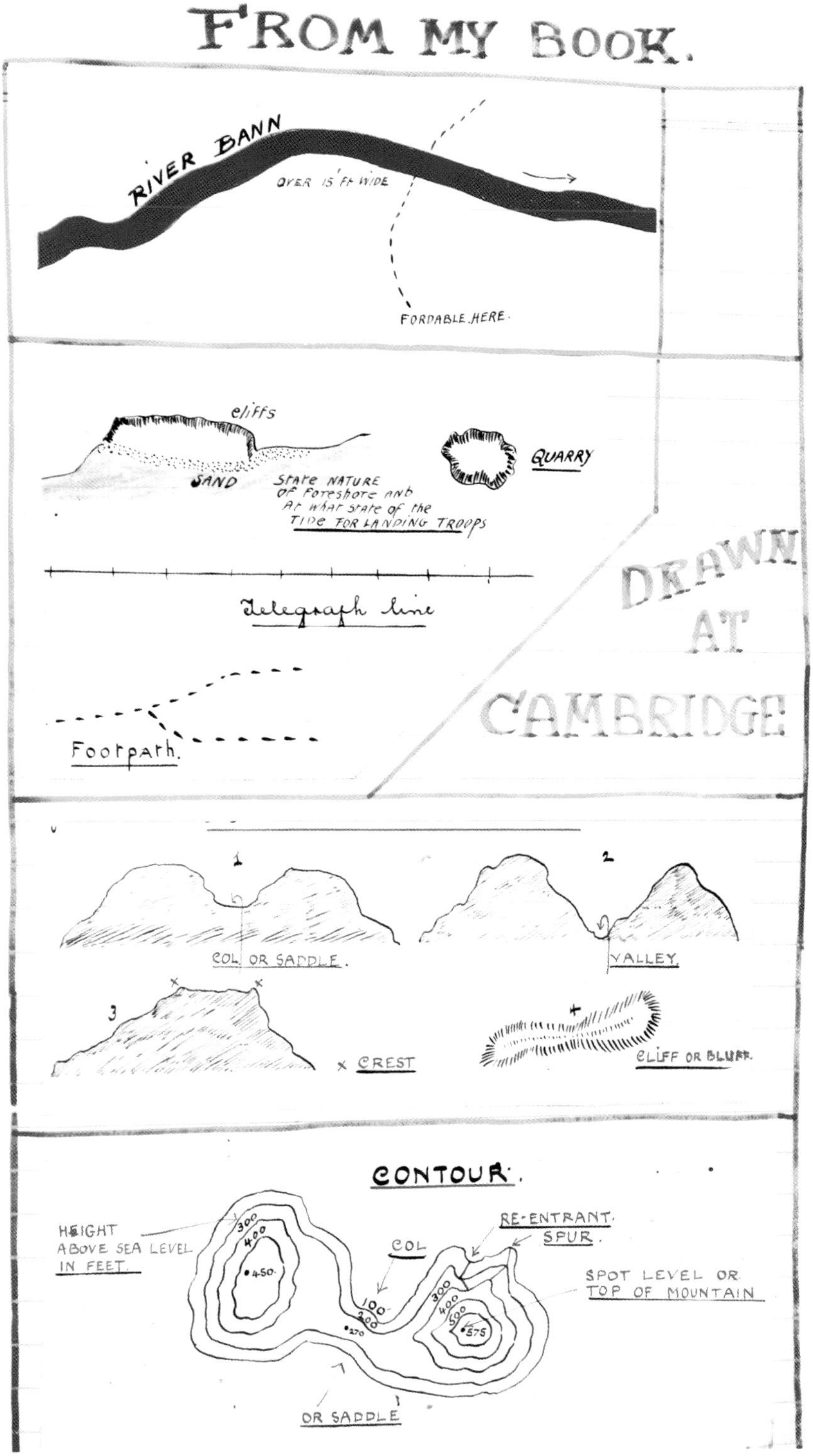

FROM MY BOOK.

RIVER BANN

OVER 15 FT WIDE

FORDABLE HERE.

cliffs

SAND State NATURE
OF Foreshore anb
At what state of the
TIDE FOR LANDING TROOPS

QUARRY

Telegraph line

Footpath.

DRAWN AT CAMBRIDGE

1

COL OR SADDLE.

2

VALLEY.

3

x CREST

CLIFF OR BLUFF.

CONTOUR.

HEIGHT
ABOVE SEA LEVEL
IN FEET.

300
400
• 450

COL

RE-ENTRANT.
SPUR

• 270

100
300
400
500
• 575

SPOT LEVEL OR.
TOP OF MOUNTAIN

OR SADDLE

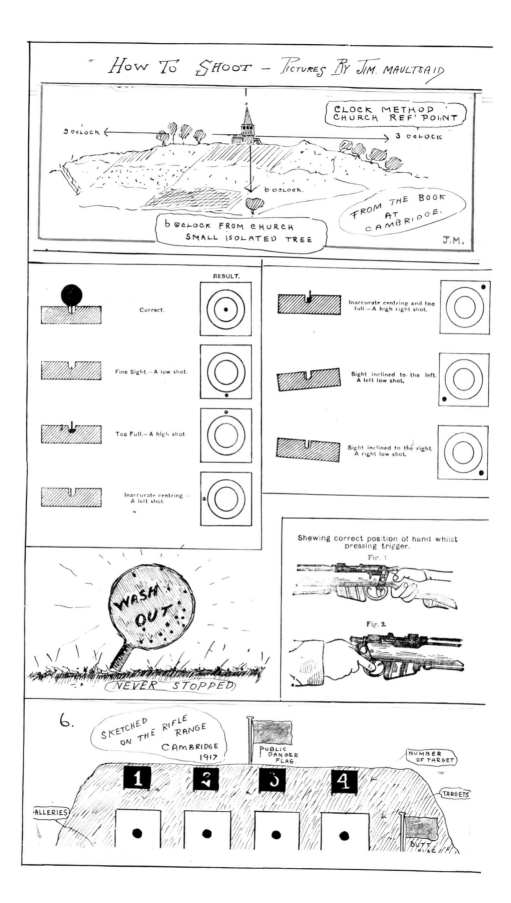

STRAIGHT

Wash out

BACK to my rookie days. Yes, straight back. How to shoot! Ye gods! Well I was a first-class marksman and shooting straight was, well, it was child's play to me. With my disability I was not allowed to do any on the range, so they gave me a job of looking after and instructing the lads who did not know one end of a rifle from the other. There was danger here and I carefully carried out my duty from the rear of the firing party. It was deplorable the frequent appearance of the 'wash out' signal.

I had a pain in my heart to see it popping up, again and again, and felt like grabbing a rifle and planting ten good shots right into the bullseye. A shock for the markers?

NO SHARPSHOOTERS

Truth to tell, I was getting bored a little with his covering ground that I had covered thousands of times already, but it had to be endured. How to take a rifle to pieces. How to aim. How to press the trigger properly. How to load up. How to … . How to … . Stop … . Stop … . My nerves are going. My only relief was the sketching of the day's work into my book – God bless that book, it saved my life times out of number and eased my feelings. The red flag for public danger was very necessary on that range as anybody or anything was liable to be shot that came within a couple of miles of Cambridge on the day that No. 4 Company were out at practice. Certainly our lot would have had great difficulty stopping a German attack on the form displayed this fine winter's morning. The sergeant instructor was reduced to tears almost, and I pity the poor soul from the bottom of my heart. No sharpshooters or snipers amongst this bunch.

HORRIBLE! Horrible! I hated this business with an intense hatred. Somehow the thought of death by gassing was, to me, just too awful for words – a curse of the age, and the curse of the Great War. How many poor creatures are still suffering from cruel gas taken in to rend and tear to pieces lungs and stomachs? I can plainly see, after all these years, those green faces, those staring eyes of man and beast gas victims of bloody war. Let there be no mistake about it: Germany had a crime to answer for, and so long as a German lives I will remember this to them: they introduced this awful method of destruction. To H★★★ with them!

SKETCHES from my BOOK

I sat and listened to the lecture but my mind was far away – this was a habit of mine these days: I simply could not help thinking backwards. Truth to tell, I learned nothing new, but just noted down a few items for memory refreshing and my examination at the end of each two weeks' study. This was a good idea, I must say – the fortnightly exam, as it gave you a chance to make a show and your marks were all carefully taken into account when the final exam was held.

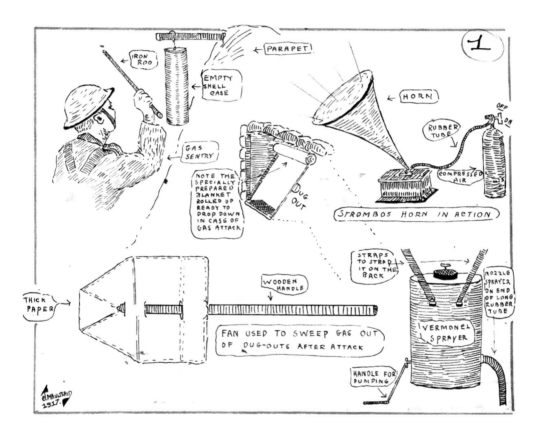

MY BOOK was by this time in great demand and assisted quite a few of the backward boys to study up certain points that they were weak in. The little pictures were especially acceptable as they had the happy knack of bringing out hidden points with greater force than any written or printed word could. The book was on loan very often indeed. I was pleased to help. On this occasion I read the noticeboard and found that our next day's work was entitled 'active service conditions', so I sat down and sketched the pictures you see on this and the previous page and labelled it 'active service at Cambridge'. I did not for

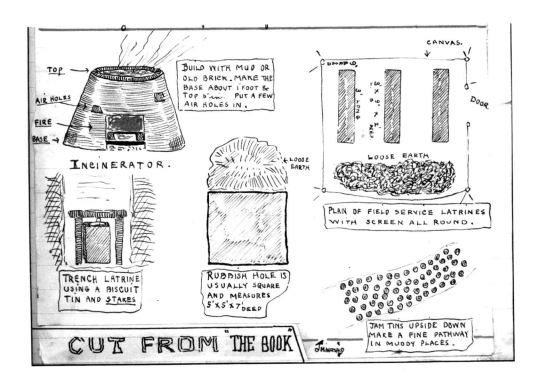

a moment imagine that my idea would receive the publicity it did but, strange to say, my platoon officer came along later that night to borrow the book and discovered that I was a day in advance as it were.

Here is the sequel. Next morning we find a dump of iron revetment stakes, shovels, tins, netting wire, old bricks, and other odds and ends all stacked up ready for our platoon to carry out to the training ground.

My pictures were all going to come to life, and they did. Incinerators, latrines, rubbish walls, duck-boards and sump holes: all were made, just as if we were in France or Flanders. I directed operations and the work carried out was splendid. Real and valuable training this, to my mind. Reality – and practice.

Pleasant times more valuable than any lecture. This was what we had learnt from hard facts of life conditions 'out there', and not found in any book.

No. 4 Company had advanced a step forward in knowledge of the requirements for Active Service from the little book by Jim Maultsaid.

PLAYING AT WAR INTO ACTION AT HITCHIN

THE GREAT WHITE ARMY

IRON rations were issued one fine winter's morning and we knew by all the signs that our trip this day was to be a long drawn out affair. In fact we were 'off' to fight a big battle somewhere around Hitchen (this is the spot famous for jam). I look back on this day as one of the best and funniest I have ever spent in the Army. It was great sport and I laughed till my sides almost split at the antics of some of my comrades. Did I say war? It was a light-hearted Battalion that took the field this day that we set forth to fight for the honour of Magdalene. We were the 'White Army' and the enemy were 'Blues', so there you are. Connecting files were put out – and they failed to connect: result – confusion. Scouts went forth and some of them did not turn up again until the next morning; others fell into the hands of the enemy: prisoners of war! Of course, a few put in some good work and reported 'millions' of Blue troops. We had not an earthly, so our scouts said.

INTO A MANURE HEAP

One lad climbed a slender young tree. It bent over with his weight and plop down he came, poor soul, to land in a dirty old manure heap. His 'observations' finished right there – but his chums shunned him for the rest of the day – poor miserable fellow.

KEEP 'IT' DOWN

We practised taking cover several times during the morning – and the famous bird that sticks its head in the sand and thinks itself safe would not have been in it with some of our fighting troops. Keep that down! Keep it flat for G★★'s sake. Flatten out!

EASY FOR THE BLUE MGs

Then the skyline was a bogey. Where were you – on the skyline, or off it? The Blue machine gunners would have had a wonderful view, I'm sure, as we topped the rising ground; only I suppose they were far too busy themselves keeping off the skyline.

THE HENROOST UPSET

How would we tackle this little farmyard? Perhaps the 'Blue boys' were holding it? My section was on the job and I gave a few quiet hints. Spread out my lads. Crawl forward along that ditch, and keep quiet. Closer and closer. Not a movement from the farmyard yet. Then some 'gaboo' upset a hen roost and such a mighty flapping rent the air – hens, ducks, and all the rest. Round the corner dashed a donkey, scared to death, and almost trampled me to death as I lay flat on my chest at a corner of the wall. Concealment now was useless. I yelled 'Charge!' We stormed the stables and outhouses. Not a living sinner did we meet. The farmyard was ours. What's this? I almost collapsed in astonishment as a sleepy cadet crawled out on his hands and knees from amongst the straw – and his cap had a Blue band on. Hands up! A prisoner. Ye Gods! A real live enemy. A scout – he would scout no more that day. He was whisked off to our platoon officer for inspection. What he revealed I know not. I do know that we were hastily mobilised and turned towards our right flank.

WHITE MICE

Now we had marched, and crawled, many miles already. It was well past midday and no grub so far. We send our outposts forward and settle down behind a hayrick to open our bully-beef tins and hard cakes. Old times! Lord! What was that? The stack almost moves. Out they rushed, scores of them – little white mice. The place swarms with these little pests. A hunt starts. War and silence forgotten. Rifle butts, big hob-nailed boots, entrenching handles, bayonets all came into action – and dozens of mice were slain – but a h★★★ of a din.

Lieutenant Hunt dashes up and raves at us. 'Stop it! Stop it all, at once! Silence!'

DEFENDING HILL 90

Fall in! We gather ourselves. Move forward in single file and line the brow of yonder hill. The 'Blues' are going to attack us. Several minutes later our platoon deploy and gradually near the top of Hill 90 according to the map.

WANTED A TARGET

Certainly a fine field of fire. A gradual decline in the ground falling away from our front, with only a skeleton wood in between some two hundred yards away. Heaven help the troops who came through those trees. Sights were adjusted. The blank cartridges rammed in – and all we wanted was a target. I was unarmed, but excited, and put myself in the place of those Wurttenberger troops who waited for us on that July morning in 1916.

ALL QUIET ...

Here they come! Don't fire yet. Indistinct forms – twos, threes and fours. Coming, coming, and not suspecting danger. Where was the shellfire? The roar of the guns was missing, and the planes overhead? All was so still. Why did the bullets not zip over and around us, and the rat, tat, tat of those ugly machine guns? 'All quiet on the Hitchen front.'

WE SAVE THE HILL

Fire! Bang! Bang! Bang! 'Rapid fire my lads.' Two hundred Lee-Enfield quick firers blazed out, and kept it up. Nothing could face this. Hill 90 is saved. The blast of a bugle says 'ceasefire'. The war is over!

WHO STOLE THE FOOTBALL POSTER?

The night before the final and it disappeared. I have indeed spent a great deal of time on this great work of art, and now it was gone. No one knew how or when. Dozens of the boys had asked me for it as a memento of our Cambridge days, but my idea was to hold a free lottery and let the winner have it.

Now on the morning of the cup final it was 'missing' and all our enquiries failed to trace it. I was sorry myself, but what could I do? Everybody suspected everybody else and I verily believe I was even suspected myself.

A WEARY JOB

It was a huge affair and every one of our team was faithfully sketched on the poster as per the sketch on page 133, a work of art, in all the colours of the rainbow – one of my best efforts in this line, and it took me many weary nights on the job. Then to think that some scoundrel had gone and stolen it from inside our quadrangle! It was just too bad. I could have cried.

TINNED MUSIC

Forget about the poster for a few minutes. Our college had got into the final of the soccer cup and the excitement was terrific. I can still remember this day as we trotted out to the beautiful playing field. Thousands of locals were present and the cadet companies mustered in full strength. Tin can bands, whistles, and horrible instruments of sound greeted our appearance.

The cup final for all England had nothing on this crowd for noise, and it was the Lord's Day. Never before, or since, had I kicked on the Lord's own day and, truth to tell, I had not much heart in this match for that very reason. I did not like the business at all.

ROUGH STUFF

I felt we would have no luck – and I was right

All the play was ours, yet we were beaten 2-1. Not a big score – but enough to lose us the match. I played hard, and played well – so the critics said – but all to no purpose. A fine game, hard and rough in parts, but I played in 'hotter' ones, so that did not worry me much, only I was not happy and glad to hear the final whistle. That was my last football match at Cambridge. Goodbye soccer! Goodbye poster! And goodbye! Lost! All lost!

THE SECRET

A few nights later we learned the secret of the missing poster. Our company commander, Major Blackburn, confessed to the stealing of this picture. We gasped in astonishment. Yes! He had gone out in the middle of the night and taken it down, for his own special collection of mementos. A cool one! What! Did Cadet Maultsaid mind it? Did I mind? … What the devil could I do? He defied us to take it back. It was his – and he meant to keep it.

THE END LOOMS NEAR

EACH day brought us nearer the end of our trials and our troubles at Cambridge. How we got down to it – some of the boys 'swotted' day and night; some worried themselves almost to death, and others did not turn a hair.

There were fifty marks for outside work (practical stuff) and fifty more for the written word. I had already gained my outdoor full marks (it was a gift to me), so did not worry overmuch. Without a doubt, we were a credit to the care and the good work of all our instructors. We had gone through the mill in fine style and now the finished article was almost at hand. Never had I worked so hard during my Army career and never was I so determined to succeed. That 'pip' was going to rest on my shoulder.

KING'S REGULATIONS

My old comrade Ward was in a bad way. He had made a mess of things on the parade ground, more or less, and was now all out to make up for this in his written examination. I assisted him as best I could, giving all my past years as background and we sat up late, often sweating and swotting King's Regulations, 'Care of Small Arms', 'Field Regulations', etc., etc. Midnight candles burned at Cambridge, tired brains reeled and tired bodies could get no rest during those hectic last days of our four month term.

The 'Day' was looming. Would all our work be in vain? Would we go back to our units in disgrace? Some were bound to fail. Would old pal Ward and I pull through? Yes! Yes! It was unthinkable now, failure! And yet? All our previous fortnightly exams were to be taken into account; our general behaviour, our bearing, our all-round fitness to be officers in more than name and uniform: officers and gentlemen.

I FALL IN LOVE

WORK from morn till night was the order of the day. Few slackers now. Some, as usual, had left things late and were in frantic haste to make up lost ground. Can they do it? I have my doubts.

Sport and pleasure had taken a back seat. Even the young ladies missed their best boys for, mind you, even during our short stay at this old world town quite a few of the lads had fallen for the local beauties. Hearts will surely be broken at the parting in a few days' time. Such was a soldier's life in war days and the girls (God bless them) had a bad time too, but the old song running on these lines … 'WE DONT WANT TO LOSE YOU … BUT KNOW YOU HAVE TO GO' sums up the spirit of the years 1914-1918. Happy, tragic years. I had fallen in love with you on my first day, grown to love you more every day, and now we are to part, perhaps forever; changes are many. I have travelled far, witnessed strange sights and scenes, but love you still, my beautiful … CAMBRIDGE.

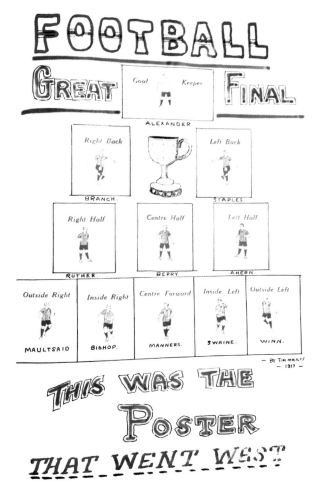

GOODBYE!

Jim Maultsaid

TO THE HAPPIEST DAYS ~ OF ~ MY ARMY LIFE

FINAL RING DOWN THE CURTAIN ON CAMBRIDGE

OUR days at the school were almost over now. The final exam was due tomorrow. There was an air of strained expectancy around us. Sadness too. Old friends must part to never meet again, perhaps! As a matter of fact I never met more than two out of the five hundred or so odd cadets that I passed through the course with in after years, so you can understand our sadness at heart. Autograph books were numerous. I sketched in scores of them during the last few days; in fact I was in great demand and my arm ached from sheer weariness. Sketch! Sketch! Sketch!

THE day arrives. We are all taken into a large hall. Each cadet has a little table all to himself. Examination papers are handed out – and the big test begins. Not a sound. Eyes scanned the questions. I run through my list and pick out the soft ones, easy ones to me. Go into them more carefully, take some rough notes, then down go the answers – for better or worse. The puzzle ones I study very carefully, and chance my arm. Truth to tell, I feel confident. Each question is now filled up – and finished. No one can yet leave the hall. I just sit and ponder over? What do you think? What Battalion would I be gazetted to? Labour Corps white, yellow, or black? Of course, I was a non-fighting category now, and it was a Labour unit for me. Not so for quite a few of my chums as we had all been medically examined some days ago and quite a bunch had been passed as A1 – for Line Regiments. Poor fellows – they had yet to face the music.

TIME is running short. Half an hour to go and the time limit would be up. Fate steps in, and careers are made or marred. Anxious faces scan the clock. Deep sighs escape – backs bent over problems that seem unsolvable, poor fellows. Time in this case is short, far too short for them. Boom! A gong sounds. It's all over now! We start up and cease work. 'Cadets 'shun! Leave your papers as they are – and – DISMISS.'

We leave that hall of memories. Outside all is in a confusion of talk. 'What the H★★★ was the answer to question number 13?' 'What did you say – and you – and you?' 'Oh, Lord, I never thought of that!' 'How stupid.' 'How silly of me.' 'Did you get number 3?' 'Yes! And you?' Such was the general run of all our talk. The noticeboard proclaimed our freedom for the rest of the day. 'Let's get away out into the town and forget all our troubles.' Much beer, I'm afraid, flowed that evening in Cambridge. Drowning their sorrows?

NEXT morning was one long to be remembered. Long lists appeared on the noticeboard in alphabetical order of the successful cadets. Of course, I crushed forward and read as follows:

CADET J. A. B. MAULTSAID   98 MARKS out of 100

I jumped for joy. Handshakes all around. Cadet Ward history today! 'Great work old man!' 'Up Huddersfield!' 'Up Belfast!' 'Officers now. Here's to good old Cambridge.' A touch of sadness also as several of our company search for their names – in vain. Such is life. All their work for nothing. I felt downright sorry, but what can I do? Perhaps it's all for the best as some of these men and boys would never have made leaders of men in this world and should never have been sent forward to a cadet school.

I could have picked out dozens of bright NCOs from my own old Battalion who would have made first-class officers with very little instruction. Indeed, later on during the war our headquarters tumbled to this themselves and picked out the go ahead lads holding one, two, or three stripes and sent them forward for commissions. This was the correct way to get the best men – men of experience, and men who could inspire confidence in the troops.

ORDERS were now issued that all successful cadets could take steps to gather the kit required as some £60 odd was placed to our credit from the pay office in Whitehall. I did not spend mine all of a rush, as some did, in buying rubbish. Hard facts guided me. I bought essentials only, as I knew that on active service it was a case of 'carry it or dump it'; also many kits had a habit of going west, so I took care not to be overburdened. I had a laugh to myself to see the kids buy all kinds of fancy contraptions. The Lord help them!

OUR LAST DAY arrives.

Railway warrants to all parts of England, Ireland, Scotland and Wales are issued. We are all gathered, drawn up in a square in the quad, and Major Blackburn gives us his final lecture and words of good advice. We dismiss for the last time, raise three cheers for our esteemed commander. Shake hands with our staff instructors. With sad hearts we crowd down to the railway station. All is bustle and hustle. Cadet Ward shakes my hand. I can see a tear in his eye. We say not a word of farewell, just read each other's thoughts. The engine whistles slowly, we move out and – CAMBRIDGE IS NO MORE (for some strange reason I was the only cadet from Ireland in this college on this course).

UNWANTED

AT VICTORIA BARRACKS, THE CURRAGH, NEWTOWNARDS

MY return journey to Belfast was uneventful. My pass read 'Report at Victoria Barracks' at the end of ten days' leave. Leave finished, I report myself. Not wanted here; they knew nothing about me, and cared less. 'Better report at the Curragh.' I trot along to Dublin, then down south. How well I remember that journey from the railway station on a cold winter's night on an Irish jaunting car away out to the barracks in the small hours of the morning to again discover to my horror that 'knowing nothing about me' was now quite the usual thing. What the devil was I to do now? Put up for the night and made very comfortable, I set out once more for Belfast. Home again! Convictions assailed me. Was I really commissioned? I sent a wire to the War Office: 'Where do I report now?' The reply was duly received: 'Newtownards.'

Good enough! Off I go. Arriving in the old town I make my way to the Headquarters of the Rifles – and was astounded to learn that no papers had come through and I did not appear on any list of officers due to report for duty.

Lord bless my heart! Here is a mess up. The adjutant sent me round to Clandeboye – and I was kept.

A regular nest of 'dug-in' and 'dug-out' officers in this outfit. I could feel that 'Kitchener men' were not welcome – and it was made pretty obvious to several of us New Army men that our stay here would be short-lived. The next draft we see our names on the list for foreign service. Nothing surer – that was the feeling I had. We must go back and see off some other faint hearts of the old gang. Of course there were men here (officers) who had never heard gunfire, except the heavy artillery practice at Kilroot, and, what's more, had no intention of ever hearing anything else if they could help it – and why should they? With such fellows as 'yours truly' available? Oh dear, no! Pop them out again, and again.

SWANK!

The Commanding Officer did not fancy us. I had now a pal from the 10th Royal Inniskilling Fusiliers (The Derrys) and, as he and I had been through the mill over there in the same old 36th (Ulster) Division, what was more natural that we should drift together – and stand alone? He was a fine big fellow, fearless, outspoken, and brave. He cared not a D★★★ for any of them. It was pathetic to see the swank and side put up at that Mess – and the bill that was presented each week would have kept you at the Waldorf in London. It cost us money. My poor 7/6 per day as a second lieutenant was hopeless. I had to draw on my reserve fund to live, and there was a war on, somewhere, but not in Clandeboye – so why worry?

SICK OF IT ALL

Together, this Derry man and I held our own, but prayed for early orders for foreign service again. We were sick of the empty swank and make-believe play of soldiers. Did I say soldiers!

BACK TO FRANCE

Called to the orderly room one fine morning after several weeks in this camp, my bright chum from the Skins and I were sent before the Commanding Officer. In a dramatic voice we were told to report at BOULOGNE in two days' time; this meant pack up and straight out, back to France. Back amongst real men again. The Lord be praised and just the two of us, out of dozens. Wonderful – wonderful.

Last two in, first two out.

That big fellow from Derry opened out and told the Commanding Officer a few home truths. I was astounded at his straight talking; he ended up by saying 'Shure and God be praised, we are glad to get away from this G★★ D★★★★★ hole!'

Up Derry! Up Belfast! And up the Ulster Division!

THE CHINESE LABOUR CORPS.
BY J.A.B. MAULTSAID.

GREAT
100,000
PICTURES
WORKS
LOYALTY
LIFE *and*

WORKERS.
VOLUNTEERS.
SKETCHES
OF ART.
DEVOTION.
DEATH.

BOULOGNE. First night in the rest camp was almost my last. A dark night and suitable for air raids. The 'Strombos' horn sounds – my tent chum and I started up! 'Come on, my lad,' I yell (he was a greenhorn – first-time out). We grab our greatcoats and beat it. Bang! Crash! zur!- zur!- zur!- zur! Jerry's engine all right, the old, old tune came back to me. Searchlights stab the sky, our guns crash out, the raid runs its course and that route was over our camp. 'All clear' sounds, and back to our tent. My chum is nervous. A strange sight meets our gaze as we strike a match and light the candle stub. Right through the tent canvas had crashed a large jagged piece of shell casing and buried itself like a knife right through three of my blankets and firmly embedded itself in the wooden floorboards just where my body should have been. Almost goodbye Jim!

IT WAS THE EXPERIENCE OF A LIFETIME

MY SERVICE IN THE CHINESE LABOUR CORPS

DID I ever in my wildest dreams imagine for a moment that I would spend a good part of my Army career as a lieutenant in the Chinese Labour Corps? I did not! And it was my own choice, on the spur of the moment to pick this branch of the Labour Corps.

I was a welcome volunteer that cold winter's morning at Boulogne as volunteers for the Chinese Labour Corps were few and far between. Some one hundred of us, all second lieutenants, lined up and each one was asked: 'Do you want to go to white labour, Indian labour, prisoner of war, or Chinese?'

I said Chinese. 'What are your qualifications?' 'None, Sir!' I answered, 'but I'll soon learn.' 'Right! Mark Lieutenant Maultsaid down as Chinese.' Thus my entry to the famous Chinese Labour Corps.

WHAT A CAREER
And what a career! Over two years of adventure, strange living, thrills, heartbreaks, happiness and wonderful experience among these sons of China.

FOLLOW ME

JIM MAULTSAID

CHINA SPEAKS

You can read it all in the pages that follow, and the little sketches (most of them sketched on the spot) will do more to give you an insight into this strange life than a thousand pages of written or printed matter ever could. Part of this section of my book was in France along with me during my travels and some of it is more or less scuffed and battered looking, but sometimes things were rather rough and conditions not altogether suitable for written pages. The incidents depicted by me are not just in routine order, but simply jotted down when the 'urge' to write or sketch possessed me, but very little indeed has been missed and the full field of our activities more or less covered.

GREAT CHUMS

And what great chums I had! Thrown together by the fates of war we were a bunch of young men out to do our best for our company of Chinese youths under our command. What pride we took in them.

How we guarded them from danger. How we fought for them, how at times we made them work like slaves, all for the 'cause', to help win the war, and how these noble Chinese boys from fifteen years upwards rose to mighty heights to please their white officers. Wonderful boys! Yes! Wonderful.

BLAND SIMPLICITY

To my last day on this Earth I will always have a very high opinion of the Chinese as people. Sober, industrious fellows, interfering with no man, only wanting to live in peace and get on with their own lives, upholding over centuries old customs and traditions. Gain their respect and esteem by honest fair dealing and you made a friend for life. Childlike in many ways, their bland simplicity often amused me and at other times their deep thinking astounded me. I set out to study their habits and language and, according to the Army authorities, became 'indispensable' in the Chinese Labour Corps.

'JUST CHUMS' (THAT'S US)

CURTAIN, SIMPSON, FORRESTER, MAULTSAID, THOMPSON

THROWN together by the whirlpool of war we five were the officers of 169 Company Chinese Labour Corps. Let me take them in the order shown above and give you a short history of each one; this will enable you to follow the stories later and assist in forming a mind's eye picture of the mentality of the officer mentioned.

I dare say if any one of them could ever read my article on themselves they would have a quiet chuckle, and say, 'Ah! It's that Irish man Maultsaid, he's always sketching or writing something.'

CURTAIN. Born in the south of Ireland somewhere and transplanted to South Africa as a baby and served through the Boer War. When the call came across the ocean he picked the 36th (Ulster) Division just to see what the North of Ireland Protestants were like, he himself being a staunch Roman Catholic. Served in our division from the early days right up to the Somme battle and got his 'knockout' at Thiepval. Was never weary telling the others how Ulstermen could fight; his opinion was placed high. Our Commanding

Officer. A strict soldier of the old order, but very fair, he was made a major before he left us for home and was pleased indeed. Offered me a job in the gold mines of South Africa; he was a mine manager himself, so this is always before me. ALL IRISH

SIMPSON. An Englishman from somewhere in Cheshire and got a smack in the wrist that finished his fighting career. Inclined to get excited for nothing. Sometimes overbearing a little in his manner and a shade too serious for my taste; used to play merry H★★★ with his platoon and servant, then would be sorry for it all. A bad way to treat the Chinese. Forrester, the Scottish boy, when well-oiled, would call English regiments by some awful names and tell poor Simpson some 'home truths' – then forget it all next morning. Simpson was in command of the company for a spell and felt his position, but I got on very well with him indeed; we worked hand-in-hand. I listened to him – then set about the business in my own way. Made a captain some time before he was demobbed. Had a sweetheart in England and wrote to her every day. How the devil she read the letters beats me – he was a hopeless writer. We kidded him unmercifully about all this writing, that's our friend Simpson. VERY ENGLISH

THREE MORE
FORRESTER gets a special article all to himself a few pages over – entitled 'Forrester' Scotch.

MAULTSAID you have been reading all about since you started this book – so I'll leave it to yourself.

THOMPSON read the story entitled 'Tommy Thompson'. What a lad! Wild West outlook – a great linguist. Tommy Thompson – a wonderful pal.

A YANKEE DESERTER?

THINKING over this incident in later days I realise now that I made a drastic error on this day. Let me tell you this story in my own way.

Marching back one day late, weary and tired out after a hard day's work, I was at the rear of my platoon when I happened to notice a figure in the long grass just off the roadside and, thinking he looked ill, dropped behind, jumped across the usual French ditch of water and made my way towards him.

He rose up and saluted. American I could see at a glance, and badly tattered too. After much quizzing, he all but admitted he was an out-and-out deserter. I pitied the boy – he was a mere boy in years, and had sampled some fighting and lost his nerve. Ran away, wandered around for days, or weeks, he knew not. He was starving now and wild-eyed, and he said he came from Philadelphia – and implored me to help him. Get him some food for the love of God.

'Oh! Please do help me, Lieutenant,' he pleaded. Soft hearted as always, it was too much for me and I then told him to lie low and I would return with a supply of 'eats', as he called it. 'Don't bring an escort for me, Lieutenant,' he pleaded as I had threatened to have him arrested. I promised not to arrest him until I had given him a meal – poor soul!

I GIVE GOOD ADVICE

Hurriedly, I made my way back to camp, had some tea, saved share of my rations, packed a small parcel of bully beef, bread, jam, cheese, a hair comb and some soap. Back along the road (a deserted spot) and he was still there, much to my surprise. He ate like a wild animal. I just sat and looked at him. 'Finished old man?' I queried. 'Yes! Sir.' I gave him a severe lecture and he promised to get back to his regiment. 'Now my boy, goodbye.' We shook hands. The last of my American friend.

BERLIN CALLING

OUR BOX BARRAGE
HUNDRED'S of GUNS
FIGHTING a RAIDER

BY. JIM.MAULTSAID.

DOWN – down – down – he zoomed. The bright searchlights held him fast in their clutches. Bombs! Guns! Crashes! Screeching of shells! The canal bank rocked and swayed.

It was a 'hot'raid. Our gun-pit, dug in the side of the canal, was hotly assailed. We were sending tracer bullets out in streams from four Lewis guns and a heavy machine gun. I was in command of this post.

Crash! Flash! A mighty roar. Hell, that was close! He had dropped one not ten yards from us. The fighting spirit had now got the better of me – my blood was on fire. Grasping a Lewis gun, I swished it round, took careful aim, rat –tat –tat – tat – zip – zip.

The big bomber swayed, staggered, side-slipped. Hell! I had it on my gun sights. I had him! Hurrah! Hurrah! My silver stream of lead was going right through him – visions of a decoration. A wounded bird now, sinking lower and lower. I curse and sweat. 'Let them rip, boys.' All five guns now belching out thousands of tracers. Swaying like a drunk man, the big black-winged bomber was in sore and dire distress – plain to be seen. We danced with excitement. What an honour for our post to bring him down. Still in the white glare of our searchlight beams. His engines were missing fire now. Yes! We had him, almost.

OUR BIRD ESCAPES

Darkness. Frantic criss-cross work by the lights. He's out of the beam, gone … gone. We wait for the crash, but, instead, ZUR –ZUR –ZUR, his engines in full running order once more. We pump lead in the direction of the sound, but somehow I feel he's clear and the sounds from his engines get fainter and fainter. Our bird has escaped – clean away. Back to German soil, if he ever made it as I feel he was a badly battered man; in fact, I knew he was on his last legs.

Did we not see our bullets going straight through his cockpit? And bouncing off the spars of his machine like hailstones? A marvellous escape. That airman (or airmen) will surely remember this night of terror over Calais, if he knew where he really was, in 1918.

Crouching down we watch and wait, but not another target for us. The raid still goes on. We hear the big bombs crash on the town and docks far behind us. B-o-o-m! Crash! Crash!

The air is thick with flying shell splinters. Anti-aircraft guns bark, big Long Toms, pom-poms,[7] all join in – in making the sky a sea of bursting shellfire. Our box barrage was at work, firing straight up to keep the raiders outside the zone – hundreds of guns in action.

THE PETROL DUMPS

Would they get the petrol dumps? Lord help us if they managed that. Millions of pounds lost and hundreds of lives, without a doubt.

FAR AWAY UP THE COAST

Gradually the shellfire dies out. White lights sweep the dark heavens. No sign of a raider left. We breathe freely once more and the night air is cool. Tired bodies slumped down beside the guns and wait the 'all clear' fog horn signal. Far away up the coast the sound of much bombarding comes faintly to our ears, from Nieuport, Ostende, Blankenberge? Then, startling in its suddenness, the fog horn crashes out, and the sound floats away up the coastline, announcing the end of one more raid.

WEARY – AND DONE UP

We shut up our post, lock the guns, and trudged wearily back – weary, weary, weary.

---

7. A light, quick-firing anti-aircraft gun. This was probably the Vickers QF 1-pounder, which was based on the Nordenfeldt-Maxim gun used by the Boers in the Second Boer War. With a water-cooled barrel, the gun fired 1-pound shells from a fabric belt that held twenty-five rounds. The term pom-pom was also given to a later multi-barrelled 2-pounder light AA gun that was used, principally, by the Royal Navy but also saw service with the Army in the Second World War.

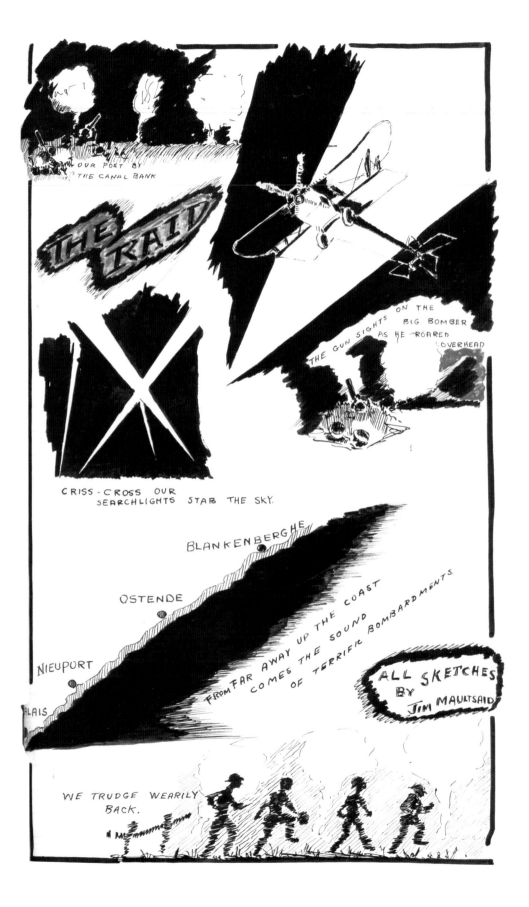

OUR POST BY THE CANAL BANK

THE RAID

THE GUN SIGHTS ON THE BIG BOMBER AS HE ROARED OVERHEAD

CRISS-CROSS OUR SEARCHLIGHTS STAB THE SKY.

BLANKENBERGHE

OSTENDE

NIEUPORT

FLAIS

FROM FAR AWAY UP THE COAST COMES THE SOUND OF TERRIFIC BOMBARDMENTS.

ALL SKETCHES BY JIM MAULTSAID

WE TRUDGE WEARILY BACK.

THE hay dump has gone up, on fire! We see the sky a red mass of flame some miles from our camp. A frantic phone message is put through to us for assistance. Cursing Jerry, hay dumps, and headquarters all in one breath, we scramble out to ring the alarm gong and see bleary-eyed white NCOs hustle dazed Chinese boys out on parade. Chinese curses mingle with ours as we gave the command 'at the double'.

I run some three or four kilometres and come within sight of a mighty blaze that almost (to our eyes) touched the sky. The heat was terrific. Frantic ASC[8] NCOs and men were dashing around giving instructions to willing helpers, both soldiers and civilians.

INTO THE CANAL

Taking stock rapidly, it struck me that the canal was near at hand and I at once ordered my platoon to go into action. Luckily the little breeze that was blowing was in our favour and we worked in fairly comfortable conditions. Buckets of water were useless, there was nothing for it but to save as many bales as we could. Each bale was wired and machine-pressed, a very solid weight for a single coolie, but the boys worked with a will, dragging smouldering bales away from the blaze. Some of them dumped their loads into the canal and this started a new line of operations. Hundreds of bales were thrown in, clouds of black smoke blinded us almost, but still the good work went on.

But our boys overlooked one very important point: we were building a dam.

---

8. Army Service Corps. It became the Royal Army Service Corps later in 1918.

FLOODED OUT

A TIDAL WAVE

Suddenly a wave of dirty canal water swished around my legs up to the knees in a second or two. Almost waist deep now. The cry went up, 'Run for your life!' What a scramble to safety. Fear from fire – now water; all that was required was a bomb or two to complete our misery. Running for life itself, we stumbled and splashed – Chinese and British all mixed up. Hissing sounds, loud explosions and the crackle of dry hay as it gave full blast to the inferno all around us. Awe inspiring, and overpowering, the heat was terrific.

ALL CORRECT SIR!

But the flow of water from the canal was doing its work as it wound its way in and around the floor of the dump – a tidal wave to put out fire, and all through a mistake. Can you beat it? Great boys, the wee Chinese! It was a job roping them all in and making sure no lives were lost by draining or burning. My platoon sergeant reported, 'All present and correct, Sir.'

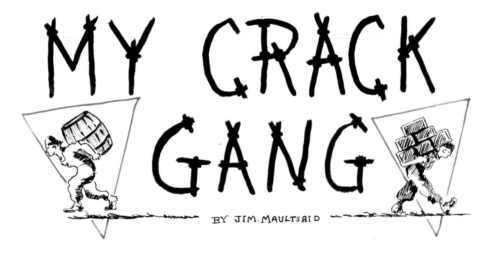

ONE of the smartest squads of colour labour in France. It was some gang, that bunch of Chinese boys. How they could work! So clever; I was often called out to demonstrate how these boys could really work when properly handled, but you must read the story.

THE BEST IN FRANCE

I WAS very proud indeed of my crack gang. Of course, I had four gangs but one lot was supreme. Willing, honest, 100 per cent workers. Could anything in France touch them?

SOME OF THE LADS

No matter what the task was, it took only a few hours until they were experts. Unloading sand; loading barrels of oil; loading boxes of petrol; loading railway sleepers and rails. Supplies of all kinds: guns, ammunition, bags of oats, coal for engines – anything and everything – glorious workers!

SIX THOUSAND BOX ORDER

See them hustle on a 'six thousand boxes order' of petrol. Chanting some strange chorus, they fetch and carry – stack to truck at an amazing speed. Hotter and hotter gets the pace. Two boxes a time now. Then three. Then four, and some of the very expert take five. Balance and poise. The sweat is running from their brown bodies.

IN ACTION

—— sketch By ——

JIM MAULTSAID.

MARVELLOUS WORKERS

The ganger himself takes a hand. Each truck is loaded exactly – and how they count beats me, but never an error. The last box is slammed home, the door is banged closed and the convoy is ready for 'somewhere on the Western Front'. Up comes the tea man, pole across his shoulders and two large tins strung on to make it balance. Squatting round in a circle, this sugarless, milkless tea is served out amid much gossip. I leave them alone. Well-earned rest; and I know my Ganger: he will not let them dilly-dally too long. That's the crack gang on patrol. Surely the best and the quickest in France?

'A SANDSTORM'

A big train of sand trucks is pushed in. Ten-ton trucks each one, and I notice they are marked L.&.S.W.R. Here's the puzzle! What can they do in this line. I make a rough calculation. One boy per truck. I strike a bargain with the Ganger: twenty-four trucks in all, twelve boys, twenty tons per boy; finish the job and go home – 'finish – a-la'. Piece-work if you like, but a big job. He looks, says 'Plenty much work', then, 'All eight' (all right). Time 8.00am. A regular sandstorm follows! Hurricane work! I am amazed. 11.00am: a cheer – or was it a war whoop?

Naked bodies almost, tumble over the sides of those L.&.S.W.R flat bottoms, grab their jackets and with many broad grins take an enormous farewell from their mates. Great work – well done!

My return of labour to area headquarters that night must have caused a flutter as I was requested to call and see the Commandant next day. But this is a story by itself, and you can read it later in the book.

OTHER DAYS ...

Numerous sketches on other pages illustrate these boys in action and no doubt you will enjoy them. Most of them drawn on the spot – something I can look back on in my old age? And think of those days – gone for ever.

THREE COATS, TWO VESTS

Now see them loading big railway sleepers! What they weighed I cannot say but know they were real heavy bits of logs.

The chain system is brought in here. Hand to hand from stack to truck – and the stack rapidly dwindles down. The sun is hot, garment after garment is thrown off one by one (some of them had several coats on, plus two or three undervests) until nothing covers the upper part of their bodies at all. Tempers are frayed as the heat is making some of them irritable. A short stoppage is necessary. My platoon sergeant finds the 'bother spot' – and the good work goes on.

SHAMED INTO WORK

One fine day I remember a strange officer from another company of Chinese come to me in distress. His platoon had struck work for some reason or other, yet this officer was a fluent Chinese speaker and was supposed to be an expert. Missionary turned Labour officer – in my opinion 'hopeless', sorry to say it. Well, I took a walk around with him and reviewed the sullen faces of his squads: glum, scowling faces.

I did not attempt to interfere or find out the cause of trouble, just said to my friend, 'Dry in for a while and leave them to me.' Calling my own Ganger, I explained to him that these boys were no use and told him to take over their work at once and show them how it should be done. The crack squad commence operations much to the astonishment of the strangers – and work like H★★★. I stand by and smile. Slowly the strikers join in one by one side-by-side with mine, and, wonder of wonders, the scowls turned to smiles. Shamed into work? Quietly, I withdraw my squad and get the strange officer. Blank astonishment! Came to me as a coolie. Smart and quick to grasp things, I watched him for a time, then gave him one stripe. Later two stripes. A short time between, and I made him ganger of my platoon – three stripes; this position of trust he held until THE END.

MR WOO, A LITTLE GENTLEMAN IN FRANCE 1917-18-19

ONE of the most perfect little gentlemen it has ever been my pleasure to meet. Attached to our company as official interpreter, he stood between us and his fellow countrymen. Educated at Oxford, he certainly was a great product of that well-known school. Perfect manners, his grasp of our language was fine, but strange to say his French was bad – indeed he could make no headway at all. Always willing to learn more about our customs and general outlook on life, in general he and I had many, many talks. I taught him lots of things, and he took great pains in teaching me Chinese.

This was my aim – to learn all I could, especially phrases that were useful on the works: words of command; how to count and all the rest of it.

I told him all about my own wonderful country, Ireland, and the glory of our mountains, our glens, our bogs, our rivers, our fairies (this last amused him, but I'm afraid he did not quite follow me as he could see I was only having a joke). I told him how the Irish soldiers had fought for England in all her wars– and were reckoned to be the best fighters in the world.

THOUSANDS OF YEARS …

Then his eyes would sparkle as he told me about his vast big country with all its teeming millions – their Gods, their customs – as old as the world itself. He regretted their lack of education and was sorry for so many of our 'misunderstandings' in our ideas of the Chinese. The strange part of it all, to my way of thinking, was he honestly believed that the white races were thousands of years behind his in civilisation. I remember one quotation of his: 'Now look here, take printing: you people think this is your own invention?' 'Yes!' 'Well,' he retorted, 'we were printing thousands upon thousands of years ago. And silk? Why that's ours too! So there you are'.

OUR NEWSPAPERS

It was a great joy to him to get our newspapers, study them all, ask me the meaning of various items and read them from cover to cover.

LITTLE FLOWER OF THE FOREST

He made great efforts to write in English, but was none too successful. I made efforts to write in his characters, but failed. In fact, I never made the least progress in this line – I was baffled. His language was too expressive for me to write: imagine saying to your best girl in this country, 'My little flower of the Forest, your beauty ravishes and prostrates me.' She would have your head tested.

MR WOO OF THE CLC

A great little fellow indeed was Mr Woo of the Chinese Labour Corps – and a great admirer of the English people.

THIS IS MY CRACK GANGER A GREAT BOY. IN FRANCE 1918.

THIS IS MᴿWOO. A LITTLE GENTLEMAN. Story on opposite page

How I made the discovery of this young Chinese boy's ability as an artist you will find on other pages, so no purpose is served by repeating the story again. Suffice it to say he was really clever with the brush and no doubt you will be greatly interested in examples of his work on the following pages. He was one of my own platoon, so I could more or less command him to do some sketching. I was careful for all that to see this side-line did not in any way interfere with his own ordinary day work. It was a spare-time occupation and, of course, his leisure hours were his own.

HIS OWN TRADE

Ching lo San was his name and, like all true artists, he was sometimes rather temperamental in his ways.

COLOUR – COLOUR

Fond of colour, his pictures were always a riot of blue, green and yellow tints, especially the last named, and, somehow or other, a soldier always crept into the sketch.

OVERTIME

When his work was 'discovered' by other officers in the Chinese Labour Corps, I was often asked to allow him to paint a picture for them and, of course, I agreed, provided they paid his price. In this way, he made a nice little sum in his spare time from his own trade – and I was of course glad.

JAZZ-JAZZ!

The dragon and his own flag always played an important part in his sketches and paintings, and the jazz decorations were startling – all the colours of the rainbow worked in somehow, truly a wonderful 'colourful' artist.

WONDERFUL CHINESE ARTIST

How he laughed when I sketched him – true to life – and how he did implore me in the name of all his forefathers to give him the picture below, but, no, I prized it so much that I kept it, and here it is today as a true memento of my Chinese artist.

WONDERFUL PICTURES

In my possession are some fine pieces of his work. These are treasured by me as far beyond price, but you have on these pages a few examples of the skill – and in a way rather unique.

REAL CHINESE ART

UNIQUE FANTASIC

THE EXPRESSION of Chinese life and culture beyond our understanding

DRAWN IN FRANCE 1918.

CHINESE ART

"IS THIS THE OLD MAN HIMSELF?"

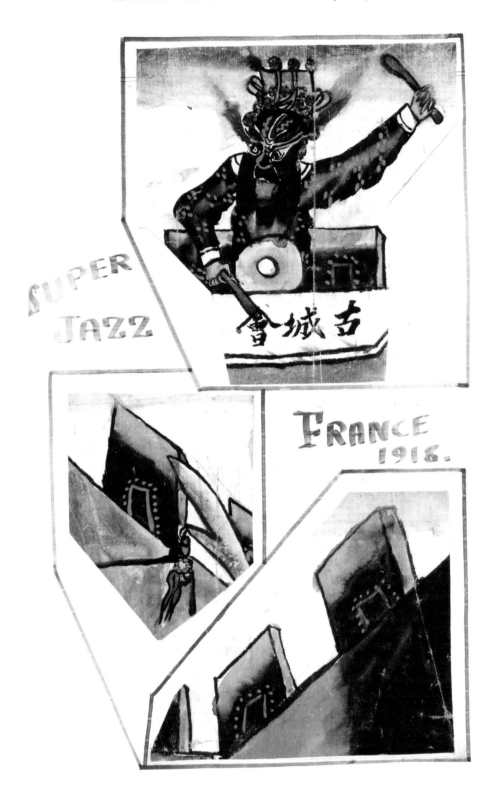

A CHALLENGE: COULD I SKETCH?

One fine day I was challenged to do a sketch of a brother officer from another company. Nothing daunted, I took up the challenge, and here below you have the result. Now this gentleman was in the printing line in civilian life and when he got my sketch was so pleased that he sent it over to London and had hundreds of copies printed – yes! He actually had thousands of visiting cards printed also – name on one side and this picture on the other.

HOW I LOST A £5 NOTE

Someday, somewhere, it was my turn to pay the wages out – white NCOs and Chinese. Once a month this duty came around. All square except a full corporal, and he was on night duty, coaling engines. The Quartermaster suggested that I should leave the Franc notes in his care; he would hand them over to the corporal when he came in. Well, I fell for it. Now the strict rule was that the officer paying out must actually hand each individual his pay, so you see I was in error. Early next morning the corporal came to me looking for his pay. I sent them to the QM. Back he came: 'Can't find him, Sir,' he reported. I was surprised.

Sending for the sergeant major, I ordered him to investigate. Hurriedly he came back. 'Can't be found, Sir! Has not slept here last night.' I got the wind up and, dashing to the Orderly Room, was astounded to find it in a state of disorder – and our cash was gone. The box contained some hundreds of French notes, our takings from the sale of refuse to the French, used as an emergency fund for food, feasts, etc. for the Chinese. Here was a fine mess. Getting through to our Military Police on the phone, I gave them the full facts and a full description of our Quartermaster friend.

Then I reported to my commander, Captain Curtain. He gave me a lecture and had a good laugh, but told me to go and pay the corporal at once, and I did. It was the best part of £5.0.0 – out of my own pay. Paying for a mistake? And no error!

"Did not wait on the dawn"

"my Quartermaster"

FLEETWOOD CALLING!

Our Redcap boys put in some fine work, and in about a week's time had the QM in 'clink'. They found him living with a French lady – on my good cash! Good! Charged with stealing funds and deserting his post, he was put away for keeps – and lost his rank. Strange to say, I was not asked to attend his trial and was in no sweet mood about it all, so it was just as well. If he had only asked me for a loan he would have got it – but the mean !!!!!!! SOME DAY I AM TAKING A TRIP TO FLEETWOOD TO LOOK FOR A FISH MERCHANT.

FORRESTER

Scottish – but ALL SCOTTISH

ALL the traditional ideas about Scots would have been shattered if only you could have known this young man – and yet he was 'all Scottish'. What a lad! What a staunch pal! And what a fine efficient officer! A left wrist shattered at Loos by a Hun bullet, he always wore a black glove to hide his white, bloodless, useless hand – poor Forrester! He had indeed suffered in the furnace of war.

BLOWING £. s. d.

A bigger spendthrift I never met, and he was Scottish! Now his pay and field allowances ran him somewhere about £17 or £18 pounds a month. That would all go before half the month was gone, then he borrowed the last part of the month from me. But wait: for some reason or other he always got a remittance from home of five, six, or seven more pounds each month. Where it all 'dried in' to beats me. £23.0.0 pounds a month gone – all gone! Up in smoke! And he was Scottish.

THE LASSIES

Of course, I know he was a lad that could lower a glass – and maybe two sometimes! And I know he would always stand the drinks all round – and pay. Oh yes! He would always pay. Then he liked and admired the French lassies (it was always 'lassies' with him) and thought nothing of taking half a dozen out to dine when he got the chance in or around a fair-sized town or village. This cost money in those days … and he was Scottish!

MAULTSAID! YOU TOSS

'Here goes Thompson! I'll toss you for a hundred francs.' 'Right,' says Tommy Thompson, 'Maultsaid, you toss the coin.' And Forrester lost. Up goes 100 francs. What a fine sport he was – wild, reckless Forrester – and he was Scottish! Such a loveable fellow.

BY THE BONNIE BANKS O'DOON

Possessed of a fine voice, he often let us have the old Scottish favourites in his own style. To hear him render 'Annie Laurie' was a treat. He had you back in Scotland with his 'You'll take the high road – and I'll take the low'. Then the 'Bonnie Banks O'Doon' was one of many sung by him, as only a Scotsman could sing it. Yes, Forrester boy – even now I can hear you sing, and all those long years have passed away. Every song ended in the 'jig' or Highland Fling, was it? He could dance, too.

CAPTAIN FORRESTER

The Chinese boys adored him. He could make them work like the devil – a hard taskmaster – but, behind the scenes, a fair honest officer of the Chinese Labour Corps. His head was screwed on properly and his brain was quick. Truly a grand officer. Taken away from us to headquarters, he was made captain, and I was delighted but missed him ever so much. Still it was to his advancement and that was as it should be. No more worthy man could have been chosen for the job on the staff.

FORRESTER

One more sidelight on this man of my story – and many characters – and I'll draw to a close.

ACROBATICS

When he was tight (drunk if you wish) he always performed a trick that none of us could ever accomplish. The trick was: placing an empty porter bottle (note the word empty) on the top of his black curly head, he caught the mess table, upended it, dishes and all (paid for the next morning), then, the table cleared, stepped up on it, stood straight up, hands by his side, then gradually sank down on his back, working the bottle slowly forward until it was all on his forehead, still standing upright. Slowly he raised his body again, bit by bit until he stood once more bolt upright – and the bottle still on the top of his head. His arms were by his side during this operation. This feat admittedly always brought the house down. The funny thing about it all was HE COULD NEVER DO THIS TRICK WHEN HE WAS SOBER.

HELL FOR LEATHER

RUSH, bustle, hustle. From the first rays of sunlight until the last bit of natural daylight faded out. March 1918. Tragic month – the Great War was almost lost in this awful month – how near we were to complete disaster the world does not even yet understand it and I suppose now never will. Black clouds hung over us. German divisions in their scores had been released from the Russian Front, owing to the collapse of that once great nation, and flung in their full force against the weak Fifth Army on the Somme front. Our General Gough was overwhelmed and his brave army 'wiped out' almost. The retreat from Mons was nothing compared to this deluge, and for some reason I never could find out why our higher command had no reserves to spare to help the Fifth Army boys.

Instead of these troops being in France and Belgium they were at home. Why? A mystery of the Great War! By the way, my own famous 36th (Ulster) Division perished in this disaster – and never were of any account afterwards as a division. Of course they 'went out' in a blaze of glory: Sir Douglas mentioned them again and again for magnificent bravery – but this is not my story just now.

PETROL

PETROL

PETROL

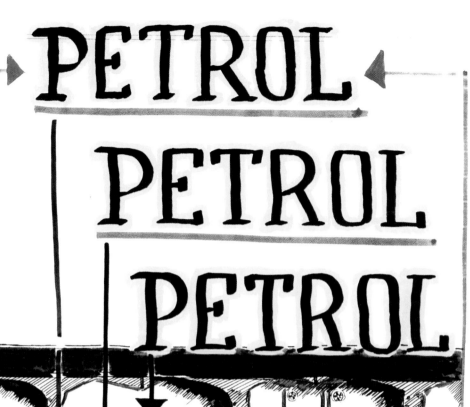

FRENCH AND BELGIAN GIRLS FILLING TINS

CHINESE BOYS LOAD UP.

FRENCH BELGIAN CHINESE

Picture a big, big shed some hundreds of feet long: in this building are hundreds of French and Belgian girls, mostly Belgian refugees. Their job is filling tins of petrol – placing them on a roller and pushing forward to the Chinese boys waiting outside. Four tins into each wooden box – and off again – the box slides forward, down the roller track, a chain of boxes now, never ending. Big trucks stand by ready for loading, and brown bodies lift the boxes one by one to hurl them inside. Stacked neatly in, at tremendous speed, each truck takes two hundred and fifty to three hundred boxes. Filled, out hop the two loaders, the section ganger marks the wagon as complete, the doors are slammed, bolted, and an empty truck is pushed in for filling. Morning till night – on, on, on. Tins. Petrol. Wagons. Petrol. Petrol. And petrol.

EIGHT THOUSAND BOXES

A big order has come in during the night hours for eight thousand cases of petrol A. Red tins for aircraft (special brand) and we are working at terrific pressure. Tins in hundreds of thousands: boxes, long lines of trucks, the chain rollers roaring in, the machinery throbbing in the big shed. Chinese boys chant in their high-pitched voices – and the sweat rolls down (on a cold winter's day). Slaves never worked like this. Even our white sergeants and corporals lend a hand. I have already given all my squads a lecture and drawn a sketch on the side of the clock of a German plane being brought down by one of ours: this was to give a demonstration of how the petrol was badly wanted. The more we loaded up, the more Jerrys would we bring down. This was a brainwave of mine – and it worked! Plenty savvy! Plenty petrol, Officer! A grin of understanding passes over the expressionless faces of my squads – and how they worked! Ah, Yes! They worked until they dropped from sheer exhaustion. We did not let our air force boys down.

PETROL—PETROL—PETROL

This is a page from my sketch book — drawn in France 1918.

MY HEAD WHIRLS
My head whirls with the strain of it all – but what matters that?

A FINE ADVERT FOR ME
Boom! Boom! Boom! Crack! Crack! Crack! Hell! What's up now?

Instinct makes me pause – and look skywards: an aerial combat far away up in the clouds. A German plane is slipping and ducking at a frantic pace as he breaks off to open out and dash for safety. We pause but for a moment, then the grind commences again. Renewed speed. I point to the sky and my gangers nod their heads as a sign of knowing what I mean. I could not have had a better advertisement than this short, sharp air skirmish.

A RACE! A RACE!
Two gangs are trying to race now! Would I act as the great judge? 'Yes! All ready? Go!' Rattle – swish – yells – boxes crash –fall from the rollers – are ignored – thrown into the wagons – some waste that could have been easily avoided – but everything is now sacrificed for speed – speed. Excitement is at fever pitch. The other gangs crowd round and cheer – or banter, I don't know, but I do know that those trucks were filled at an amazing rate. My crack gang wins easily – by five or six boxes – and the whole squad of twelve coolies just flop down on the ground for a breather. 'Good work boys!' (Ding hola), 'but no more racing today. Steady does it. Come on – up and at it again.'

Tins – tins – boxes – boxes – petrol – never ending.

'WONDERFUL 169'
A little rest at 10.00am, some hot tea without milk or sugar then back to the toil again. By midday we had over five thousand boxes loaded up – this was fine going and the order was in sight of being completed.

LEAVE IT TO THE FRENCH AND BELGIANS
An argument between some Belgian girls and several of my own bright sparks had to be fixed up. In my broken French (very broken), some English and Chinese, I cooled the frayed tempers by soft speech, getting the 'works' going once more. It was a work of art keeping them all going, hot tempers on the French and Belgian side and stubbornness on the part of my lot. How those girls could work! Experts all – they could move at a terrific pace – and seldom, if ever, did the machinery break down. Of course they were on piece work and when it comes down to hard cash you can leave it to the Belgians and French.

WHIRLING ROLLERS
'Come on One Six Nine!' I yell! Faster yet! Boxes slide down the rollers – are caught and thrown into the trucks. Crash! Crash! Whirr! Whirr!

'FINISH A LA'
Working like madmen are 169. The evening is wearing down as we grind down these never-ending lines of boxes – boxes – boxes.

'E, EY, SAN, SIR, WOO'

Down to the last five hundred cases. Two wagons are pushed forward for this consignment. Tired hands are thrust forward and the last lap commences. 'E, EY, SAN, SIR, WOO'(1-2-3-4) chant the markers as the boxes are hurled forward – competition is fierce for the honour of first finished. No trouble in urging the boys forward.

GREAT WORK

Finish a la! Finish a la! The end, in English. I smile and answer, 'San gowdy. Ding hola.'

My two thumbs go up, Roman fashion, and it's all over for another day. And what a hectic day too! No shortage of petrol tomorrow for our aircraft. I feel delighted at our great work, knowing in my heart how they depend on us – us, on the 'lines of communication' – for supplies. Dog tired, we gather our squads and march out for a few hours' rest (perhaps) in our camp some kilometres away. My head sinks on my chest. Asleep on my feet.

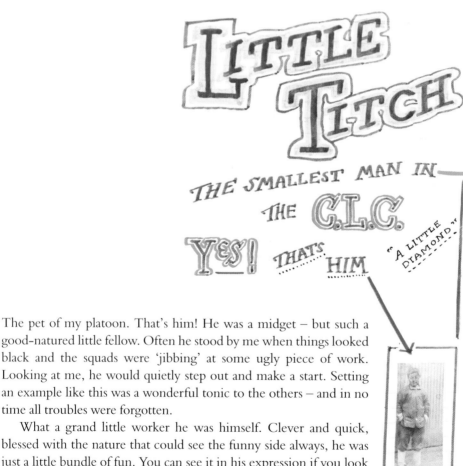

The pet of my platoon. That's him! He was a midget – but such a good-natured little fellow. Often he stood by me when things looked black and the squads were 'jibbing' at some ugly piece of work. Looking at me, he would quietly step out and make a start. Setting an example like this was a wonderful tonic to the others – and in no time all troubles were forgotten.

What a grand little worker he was himself. Clever and quick, blessed with the nature that could see the funny side always, he was just a little bundle of fun. You can see it in his expression if you look at his photograph. He was older than his looks, yet not old, I knew. His age? I don't know.

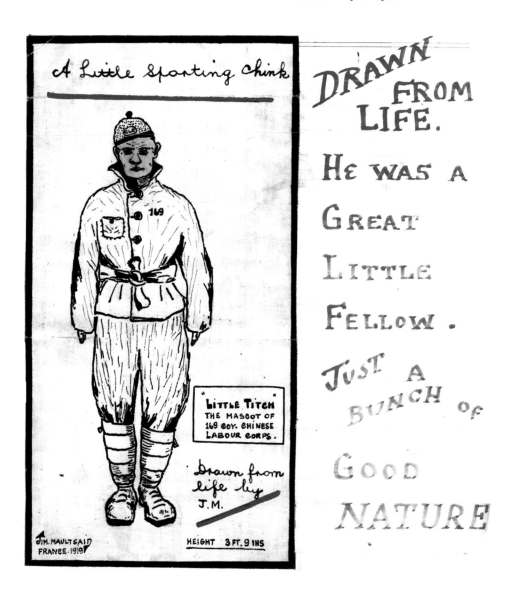

A Little Sporting Chink

DRAWN FROM LIFE. HE WAS A GREAT LITTLE FELLOW. JUST A BUNCH OF GOOD NATURE

"LITTLE TITCH"
THE MASCOT OF
169 COY. CHINESE
LABOUR CORPS.

Drawn from life by J.M.

JIM. MAULTSAID
FRANCE.1919

HEIGHT 3 FT. 9 INS

A POCKET SANDOW

To see him stripped from the waist up – you got a shock. The muscles rippled under his brown skin. How they stood out when he was at his work. A powerful back and shoulder development gave him amazing and undreamt strength. A pocket sandow!

HIS PIPE

He was fond of his long pipe – smoked often and hard. This was his only weakness, if you can call this a failing.

171

'NO GOOD A LA'

I asked him several times to take a stripe – but would he? 'No good a la, officer,' – was the reply. I looked surprised and said, 'Me no good a la? 'Oh! No! No! No! Officer good! Stripe no good a la!'

A FAVOURITE

Apart from being a favourite of the officers and NCOs, he seemed to be very popular among his own race too – surely a good sign?

JACK AS GOOD AS HIS

Visiting 'red caps' looked at him in wonderment. Was he put out? Not him. He just bowed in his own peculiar manner – smiled, and carried on.

    A wonderful lad was 'Little Titch'.

'BABOON'

HELPLESS? HOPELESS

THE strangest character in our company was the 'baboon', as we called him. If ever a human being verified the theory 'down from the apes', here was a living example. Devoid of brainpower, he just ambled around and tried to imitate his companions at work; he tried to do as they were doing, not often with much success. Talked all the time to himself, or, should I say, muttered, in a strange lingo unknown to any other Chinese man.

    His squad took turns to feed the soul as he was unable to feed himself. Matted hair, face without a spark of intelligence and long powerful arms hanging far below his knees. From enquiries I made, he came from somewhere up in the wilds of Siberia – no one exactly knew where. A truly amazing character, we always treated him like a child as he was quite harmless. His companions were all kind to him also and, as far as I could judge, he was quite happy in the CLCs.

He was surely on the verge of sixty years – and he had fallen in love with a beautiful fair-haired Belgian refugee. Belonging to the Australian forces, and now in the ranks of the Army Service Corps, he was attached to the big petrol dump outfit.

A d***** botheration, I ranked him. Suspicious, always watching the movements of this ladylike girl. I got tired looking at him 'mousing' around where he should not have been and told him to keep clear of the depot. This man should have been (and was, I suppose) an old grandfather – and he was acting the fool during business hours.

I would have bet, too, that his wife in Australia would have got the shock of her life if she could only have had the chance of watching him for a day or two. The old!!!!!

AN ORPHAN

At first I was amused at his antics. Then I became alarmed. In deadly earnest he became a menace.

And the girl herself?

I stopped one day and had a conversation with her. She had lost father, mother, brothers and sisters all in 1914 in Belgium. Her parents were shot down by the d*** Hun. Forced to flee for her life, she somehow escaped and had, up to now, supported herself. Well bred, without a doubt, I felt sorry for her. She certainly was a lady, and a real 'blonde beauty' too! Out of place, I thought, mixed up in a mob like this – but as she said herself she 'had to live somehow'. I mentioned the old Australian. A look of horror and pain passed over her face.' Oh! I hate him, he's horrible. And his eyes! They hold me down, in his power. How I hate him.' This talk was all in English. Her English was splendid. A convent upbringing?

'Look Lieutenant!' Round the side of a wagon, not twenty yards away, were those dark, arrogant, piercing eyes – watching us: hate, malice, envy.

WATCH HIM

'Be careful, miss,' I say, and walk away. I keep my shooting iron (revolver) butt handy in case of a quick draw, for I would not put it past him attempting. The old ruffian.

HAUNTED HER

He still haunted her. Her life was one long terror from this undersized old man who was determined to possess this fair flower of Belgium – and possess her he eventually did; at least, so far as I can gather, he 'got her' in the end. Yes! Got her.

DOWN TO …

Having been ordered further afield, I lost all trace of this depot for quite a while, and when I did return I heard the news that he had made her marry him, and she had a dog's life since that date. And I quite believe it. I pitied the poor lass in the hands of this vampire – but I could not interfere. I always felt that it would not have cost me a moment of remorse the planting of a revolver bullet in that old man's stomach. He was a human vampire – and brought this girl down to despair, and worse.

Ordered down to a big railway siding one day to unload sacks of oats, we had hardly got started when a long train pulled in – and the train was a Red Cross one, for horses – poor dumb animals – all wounded in the war. What a sight to see them lying in those vans, all cut and wounded. Their eyes held a tragic note – somehow a horse can tell you a lot by its eyes. The poor beasts had suffered and were still suffering.

WOUNDED HORSES INDIANS AND TAUBE'S 10 MINUTES HORROR

WHAT A WAR!

Their attendants were Indians. Long beards, thin brown bodies, thinner legs, light coloured puttees and long thin hands. This was my fleeting impression of these sons of India. The train stopped opposite us. How my Chinese boys stared. What kind of men? What country from? What are they doing in France? What? What? Dozens of questions were flung at me. I had to smile to myself and the thought flashed through my head: what a funny war!

BLINDING FLASHES

Crash! Blinding flame. Crash! Confusion. Horror. Wild horses, mad with fright. Hell – and hellfire! Cries and shrieks of pain. In the name of G★★ what is it? Plunging bodies, kicking iron-shod feet – what a shambles. The roar of aero engines far overhead. Swish! Crash! Earsplitting thump! The ground shakes. Up goes a truck in a sheet of flame. Stifling fumes choke us. I yell, 'Take cover.' My squads hurl themselves beneath the big French trucks for cover. I crouched down too, and awaited death. C–r–u–m–p! The very rails seemed to bend. Showers of hot metal flew past. My heart was pounding. I grasped a frenzied Chinese boy and hurled him down again as I threw myself flat down, and awaited the end. C–r–a–s–h! I heard it coming – or I thought I did. This was as hot a raid as I ever had the misfortune to pass through. I'm candid enough to say I was afraid – but had to show a brave face before my Chinese boys.

ETERNITY …
Eternity seemed to spread its wings for me – ages and ages pass, and re-pass. What a horrible death!

THOSE TAUBES
'Jerry' passes over. The storm has passed. Thank God! I look at my watch. What a funny thing to do – and I see we had some ten minutes of 'red hell'. Those Taubes are a terror, not to be despised. And their bombs! Deadly, and destructive.

MAD HORSES
White, scared faces. Indians and Chinese still peered out from below the trucks. I emerged, and ordered them out. Slowly they obeyed me – and gradually our shattered nerves calm down. The raid was over. Horses still mad with fright were plunging about the railway siding – we all lent a hand to subdue them. One truck load was a horrible sight – legs, but why describe it? The poor animals will suffer no more.

PROVIDENCE
I order a roll call for both the Indian troops and my lot. Wonder of providence! All present!

GOODBYE PIGTAILS

I cannot say if it was an official order, or just a fad, but all the pigtails had to come off – my! It was a wonderful sight to see them in hundreds being cut clean away. Some great heads of long black coarse hair, like a horse's tail hair that reached far below the waist and as strong as wire. Some of my boys kept their as a treasure but most of them threw them away.

SNIP-SNAP
The Chinese barber had a busy time and thoroughly enjoyed it all: snip, snap, snip, snap, off she comes! A great many then had a style of hairdressing all their own, unlike anything I have ever come across since.

POOR JHONNY CHINK LOST HIS PIG-TAIL WHEN HE LANDED IN FRANCE.

PIONEERS OF THE 'BOB'?

Shaved clean as could be right up to the ears – and right across the back of the head a tuft was left about the size of a bowl all over the top of the skull – see the little sketches. Funny looking? I sure did have a laugh to myself.

Of course, some of them had more up-to-date ideas and had a cut like the Europeans – quite posh fellows in a very short space of time too. Oh, yes, lots of them did not at first like the idea of losing their hair, but 169 Company were all in due course shorn of their locks and looked 100 per cent neater after the operation. Strange to say, I never knew a fair-haired Chinese man – all were dark haired. A heritage of their beloved China? I WAS AMUSED.

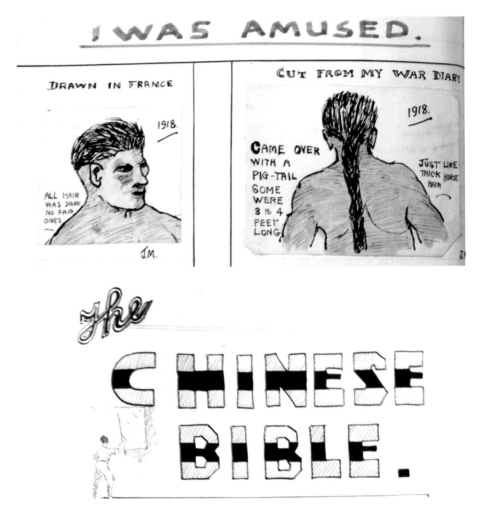

So far as I could gather the Chinese boys did not trouble overmuch about the question of religion. I know, of course, they had their own strange Gods, many idols and many rites – but, truthfully to me, they were more or less rather indifferent. Our Labour Corps Headquarters had a Chinese Bible issued and each company got a supply – you can study it

Chinese Bible.

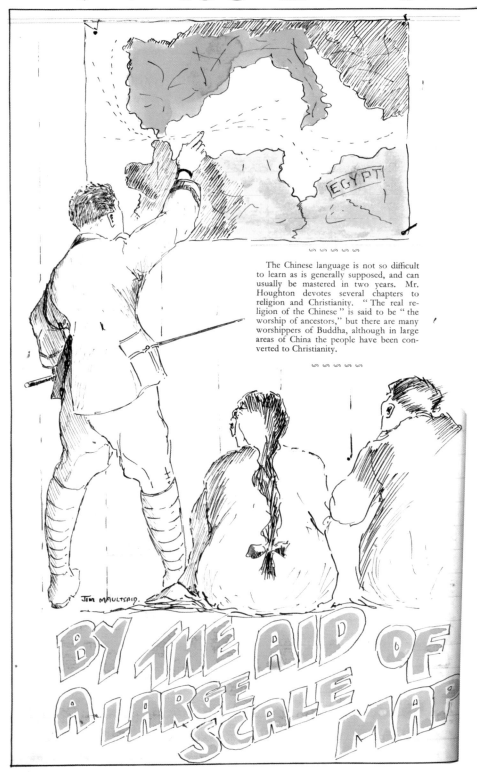

The Chinese language is not so difficult to learn as is generally supposed, and can usually be mastered in two years. Mr. Houghton devotes several chapters to religion and Christianity. "The real religion of the Chinese" is said to be "the worship of ancestors," but there are many worshippers of Buddha, although in large areas of China the people have been converted to Christianity.

JIM MAULTSAID.

BY THE AID OF A LARGE SCALE MAP

INTERESTING PRINT

PAGES CUT FROM THE CAINESE BIBLE. CAN YOU READ IT

a few pages over and see what you can make out of it yourself. This is what we officers were faced with! How would you have tackled it? I secured a large-scale map of the Holy Land, got my friend Mr Woo, then, armed with a walking stick and a picture of 'The Cross', I made an effort to tell them that old, old story of how He died for us.

ENJOYED THE BIBLE

Don't misunderstand me. We officers were not supposed to teach the Bible – that was the Padres' job, but I had a brainwave and, of course, when I had one of these it had to be tried. My first lesson was enjoyed. All the signs pointed that way, so said Mr Woo, but to say it was understood – well, I won't say that.

Let it be as it may, I was asked to read them, and tell them, some more of my wonderful stories. My word, I was pleased! Simple as children, I put it to them, and taught them about their wonderful Father in Heaven, and mine too. This seemed to cause a great deal of discussion; Mr Woo himself was a Christian, and this helped me a great deal indeed.

My lessons of Bible history took place only amongst my own platoon of course, and I can't ever recall Simpson, Forrester, or Thompson giving their squads any of these lectures. I only hope and trust that some of my teaching bore fruit, as some of them could have been doing with a bit of knowledge. 'Little Titch' was always deeply interested – and seemed to grasp it all.

THE FURTHER BACK ...

Chinese funerals were rare affairs. You can read later in the book how they made provision for the spirit etc., etc. Great believers in their great-great-great grandfathers, each and every one of them believed that they themselves were the 'spirits' of long dead and buried friends. Father of my father! Come back – living again – in them. Do you follow me? Strange to say, their swear words also raked up their great-grandfathers too – and the further they could go back the more effective was the 'swear word'. Strange!

The leaving of this world was only the commencement of the journey and in time the 'spirit' was sure to return in some shape or form, or enter the breast of someone.

These observations are only my own and may not be all correct but, from my experience, are more or less the main idea of their religion. Some of them, poor fellows, were out and out heathen, but for all that will surely find a place in the 'Hereafter' as they were far and away better men than many of the white ones I knew.

LIFE IN THE CLC

As I said before, in my humble opinion, many of these companies were very badly handled both by officers and white NCOs who lacked the ability to realise and understand that the boys were all volunteers and human beings like ourselves. The PoW (prisoners of war) attitude was all too prevalent and the CLC were not that. Thank goodness our 'skipper' was a man of great good heart, fine understanding of human nature and placed much faith in his lieutenants, not one of whom let him down. Without the least spirit of boasting I still say that our 169 Company was one of the very best in the Chinese Labour Corps.

A STRANGE FANTASTIC LIFE

JIM. MAULTSAID.

OH! WHAT A HOLIDAY

It was a Chinese holiday, and the boys, just like all the boys in the wide world over, made up their minds to have a bit of fun – I was interested of course in the programme of events, but for the moment we will only talk about the stilt-walking display. As a youth I had a shot at this sport but I can tell you at once my eyes were opened when these boys appeared on their long legs to treat us to a most marvellous display of stilt walking.

EXPERTS

Some were ten, fifteen, twenty feet up – and their legs were strapped to the stilts; think for a moment what a fall meant! Dances, competitions for high kicking, musical turns, various evolutions were all gone through in great style, and a single tumble. Of course they were experts all; strange to say most of them were from my own lot and it amused me to see Leo Fen Seo or Ling Fen hopping merrily around – better at this than work! The lads you see in actual photograph are my own platoon in action. This picture appeared in a Chinese journal.

STILT WALKERS

The Chinese spectators were interested greatly themselves and enjoyed the fun. A wailing tin whistle played on and on, and the dancers had 'clappers' in their hands; others carried a long pole for balance. Huge masks of weird and fantastic designs adorned several 'unknowns'.

DANCING

A few wore long dresses or gowns right to the ground almost and looked like giants towering far above us on the sky line; to have a rest they sat on the edge of the huts and took a breather. Their folk dancing was a sketch – round and round, in and out, backwards and forwards. The comedian of the show was 'Little Titch', on a very small pair of heavy stilts. He caused endless amusement – and would dash between the legs of a very tall companion time and time again. He was a turn! White-faced, green-faced, yellow-faced monsters strutted around, all doing their best for the show. I shall long remember the 'stilt walkers' of the Chinese Labour Corps in France.

THE STILT WALKER

NOTE THE MASK WORN.

JIM. MAULTSAID
1918.

BLACK

(A WONDERFUL STORY)

— ART ?

A terrible plague sweeps over our company. *

SLEEPY sickness or flu, or a yellow plague? I know not, but a strange illness came over our company – and the boys were dying fast – good boys too. Too good to lose. We were at our wits' end to get to the bottom of it all, but our own white Medical Officer seemed to be baffled. Some dropped down on the works, were carried home, and died. Some lay sick for a few days, then passed out to meet their Forefathers. I had by now lost half a dozen of my very best workers. I tended them and cheered them up, and often spent all night long by the bedside of a poor soul who was 'going west'.

'Take my hand, Officer'. A mute appeal, glazed eyes, a gasp – and he's gone! The disease appeared to affect them thus: no life, energy, seemed stupid, or doped in the morning, and before the sun set – dead.

THE MEDICINE MAN WORKS BY CANDLE-LIGHT. I WATCH THE OPERATION

— JIM. MAULTSAID 1918.

NIGHTMARE DAYS

Several nightmare days and nights had passed when one night I was awakened from a heavy sleep by my boy (or servant): 'Wake up, Officer!' Being well used to sudden alarms – I was wide awake in a flash, what's wrong? Number Two Ganger wants you Officer. Hurriedly I pull on my big boots and rush out, to be greeted with a 'follow me' in Chinese. My Ganger was excited, and so was I. What the devil was wrong now? Grasping his arm I followed him through the darkness and was led to our platoon hut.

A single candle light is shining. We pass down between the rows of sleeping bodies in towards the light. Then a strange sight met my gaze …

THE OPERATION

An old Chinese man was performing a strange operation, on one of No. 2 Platoon. I watch, fascinated: a long needle threaded with yarn (?) was run through the skin of the patient in the grip of the 'scourge' – five times in all, in a strange design, on the left side of his chest; like this ⠪; that was all. In …out … five little wounds.

The old witch doctor (?) murmured 'plenty work', meaning he (the patient) was going to live and do lots of work for me. I hardly knew what to do. Report the matter – or wait and see? I waited. That boy lived and recovered. Auto – suggestion? What you like! Or maybe witchcraft – but he LIVED. Good enough for me. I kept my secret. Dozens of my boys were treated with the magic needle – and all got well again. The plague dies down in my platoon. Should I tell my captain and brother officers? Still I hesitated; but, strange to say, fate decided.

THE OLD MAN DIES

About a week later I was again called to an urgent case – just as the day was wearing done. 'Come quickly! Qua – qui! … the old man dies.' To his bedside I hurry. Yes! It's the old 'medicine man' himself, and going fast I can see, from the 'dreaded disease'. Oh! Lord … poor old fellow. I stand and gaze down. He whispers, 'Officer, Officer.' Bending down, he takes my hand and signs to me – the needle … his magic needle: would I operate on him? My throat is dry. Tears come to my eyes. Oh! I dare not. I could not … it would never do. His spirit goes to join others in those realms beloved of Chinese men. I loosen his fingers, cross his arms across his chest, pull the blanket over his old wrinkled face, step back – salute.

I kept my secret for these pages.

"THE" GHOST OF 169.

The coolies were restless. By now I had gained enough knowledge of the 'lingo' to know that. What was the trouble? All is not well. Taking my own boy I put him through 'the third degree' and was astounded to learn that a 'ghost' haunted our camp and was generally in or around an old outhouse in a corner of the compound.

Not being much afraid of spooks – had I not seen them in the front line? I took my six-shooter and set out to investigate. The wind howls, it's a very wild night. Tall willow

HERE'S THE GHOST ?

SKETCHED *IN* FRANCE. 1918.

trees bend and sway. The rain slashes down. Curse those trees – how they creaked. I shelter from the storm by the side of the old outhouse. An hour passes: no earthly, or unearthly, form appears.

About to give it up, I was almost startled out of my wits as a form rustled past me. I could hear it take a deep breath. Good! Only human. Out goes my gun. I jam it into the back of – a startled Chinese man!

Flashing my electric torch in his face he almost collapsed with fright. 'What the H★★★ are you doing my lad?' 'Nothing Officer! Me come lookee look for spirit gone away!' 'Gone where?' 'To his great-great-grandfathers.' 'Cut it John, what's the trouble?' Clutching my arm, the Chinese boy leads me to the door of the old hut and, pushing open the door, whispers, 'Look! Look!' I flashed my lamp. A body is swinging in the breeze, hanging from a beam by a puttee. The ghost! I shut the door and leave my companion back to his hut. Cut down next morning, the body was over a week old; and it was his brother who had led me to it. Poor fellow, he was hoping for a return of 'the spirit'. Finish – a – la!

THE SWORD SWALLOWER. NO STAGE TRICK THIS A REAL AFFAIR.

You have read about these sword swallowers, and like me have put it down to a trick? Oh, yes, you know how it's done – a spring that contracts when pressed in! Well! It may be this – on the show halls – but let me tell you about a real 'sword' and genuine performer.

LEATHER THROAT
Short, broad-chested, he looked a real athlete, and was all that. A throat like leather and his skin the same deep tan, he was swarthy to a degree that was almost black. And his hair was almost curly. Strange!

THE SWORD

No one could say he did not look the part. His sword was a weapon some fifteen inches long; but it was not sharpened – just blunt edges. Still it was solid.

DOWN ... INCH BY INCH

We rest at the dinner hour. Someone suggested he should give us a turn. Nothing loath, he agrees to do so.

Lying down, he rolls over and over on his side – and leaves behind him a long strip of thin carpet material that has been wound around his body like a window blind (roller pattern). Cute? Several quick handsprings – cartwheels – no hand touched the ground – and he ends up bowing to us. From somewhere the sword is produced. Bowing low, he opens his mouth and, slowly bending his head back until I thought his neck would break, he gets his proper position.

The sword is poised aloft, then the point is placed in his mouth And down it goes ... inch by inch, until only the handle is left. Turning around, he lets us see for ourselves how real it is – and slowly withdraws. We give a hardy handclap. It's a real good trick. Throwing the sword high in the air, he catches it, by the handle, as it nears the ground again and the trick is completed. Bowing low, as only the Chinese can, he smiles and claps his hands.

ROUND AND ROUND

Little Titch steps forward, is grasped, turned upside down and stiffened out. Slowly he raises him until he has him at arm's length above his head, then he jerks the little body into the air catching it by the feet as he falls, and swings him round and round in a mad swirling movement, to throw him some six or seven yards away. He alights on his feet. 'Titch' looks relieved to get it all over, and I don't blame him.

TRY THIS YOURSELF

His next trick? Taking three French pennies, he places them all flat on the carpet, 'heads' up, and, balancing another one carefully in his long and first fingers, he throws it high up into the air. Down it comes to strike the three coins on the ground – and all four pennies lie flat, 'tails' up. Could you do it? Just try!

SHOWMANSHIP

I often got him to do his stuff for visiting 'red caps' etc., much to their amazement and delight. He was a real showman and acrobat.

ALL DRESSED UP TO GO OUT ON PASS - SOME OF THE RAREST TURN-OUTS YOU EVER SET EYES ON. SWALLOW TAILED COATS WERE FAVOURITES BLACK STRIPED TROUSERS AND TALL BLACK HATS. MY !!

JIM MAULTSAID

AN OLD FRENCH TOPPER. RED TROUSERS. COLLAL ABOUT 6 INCHES HIGH ELASTIC SIDE BOOTS. COMPLETE WITH WALKING OUT CANE. A SCREAM!

J.M.

THE USUAL "TURN OUT" WHEN OUR BOYS GOT THEIR UNIFORMS AND PROPER BEARINGS.

J.M.

THESE PICTURES are all from my war diary.

BATTERED SOFT FELT HAT. RED JACKET. OLD GREEN PANTS. AND BROWN BOOTS. GEE WHIZZ!

in France with the C.L.C 1917-8-19.

J.M.

YE GODS!

THE pictures on the opposite page will give you some idea of how our boys turned out on Sundays in their early days in France. Later on they became more conservative and more or less stuck to their own uniform. These pictures are not in any way farfetched; drawn on the spot, everyone is correct to the last detail. You cannot fail to agree with me when I say it took us all our time to keep from bursting right out – with laughter! I almost collapsed.

ELASTIC SIDE BOOTS

After a few weeks in this foreign land their ideas underwent a change, and lots of them made deals with the French civilians – the results were startling, as you can see.

Now for good work and quiet behaviour we granted them a 'pass out' from the compound on Sunday afternoon (when we were not working) and I was startled one day to see one of my leading lights turned out as follows: French tall hat, red trousers, elastic side boots and, to crown it all, a collar about six inches high! My! It was a scream.

Did I turn him back? Oh no! He deserved a medal, and I had not the heart to disturb his serious face.

I would have paid £5 for a camera, but they were not allowed.

This rig-out started a fashion in our company and the following Sunday was long to be remembered. Here's a few samples of the full dress turn-outs.

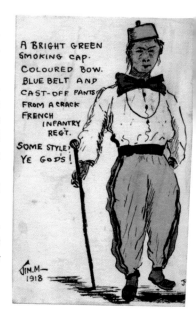

A BRIGHT GREEN SMOKING CAP. COLOURED BOW. BLUE BELT AND CAST-OFF PANTS FROM A CRACK FRENCH INFANTRY REGT. SOME STYLE! YE GODS!

JIM.M— 1918

RED JACKETS

An old battered soft hat, bright red jacket, green trousers of large and airy dimensions, brown boots, and a fancy walking stick, plus gloves of a white colour.

A sight for the Gods! ... and us.

DING HOLA!

Picture a bright green sort of pillbox, or smoking cap, below that a pure starched white shirt, complete with an old time dickey and a big red and blue tie made up in a long bow. Blue belt, and a pair of old French cast-off infantry pants that still had their stripes sewn on down the side of each leg. Surely this outfit would have been worth a fortune to our own 'brighter dress reformers?' 'Ding hola.' Good!

MONEY FOR JAM

Some of the cute French people must have made money from these simple Chinese boys of ours as you could see that these were all old rubbish raked out from the lumber room, or scrapheap, and palmed on to the innocent Chinese!

THE CRAZE DIES

Thank goodness the craze did not last long and soon died out, to be replaced by smart neat uniforms all washed and cleaned, especially as we were particular in 169 Company and passed each one by inspection before they got out for a walk on Sunday afternoon.

But the fancy dress turn-outs! I can laugh yet, when I remember.

RUM –TIDDLE – TUM!

Tum – tum – tiddle, tum! Tum – tum! Screech – screak – screech. The big show is full steam. This was the festival of 'the moon' (to worship the moon). Two whole days were given up to this festival and part of the programme was a theatre show in Chinese. Without a doubt it was a wonderful display and officers of the company were all invited; we had front-row seats in the open air and got a close-up of the stage.

TWELVE COURSES

First of all we had to take part in a meal, of about twelve courses; what they were made out of I cannot say, but eggs that were green with age, worms and snails, rich spices and sweetmeats all had a place on this mysterious menu. Gee! My stomach revolted, but I had to make some sort of show, and not give offence, so I nibbled a little, and bluffed a lot, and managed pretty well indeed. Lord bless me, I can even taste it yet!

DRAGONS

The stage is built at the side of a hut, big curtains all covered in fearsome designs (dragons etc.) stretch all along the front and up to now no eye has caught sight of the actual stage props. Crash! The orchestra bangs out (their picture is on the next page), the curtains move back and their show commences. The bold bad man struts on, armed with a big double-edged sword and a massive false face. He looks the part. What it was all about was beyond

HE LOOKED THE PART

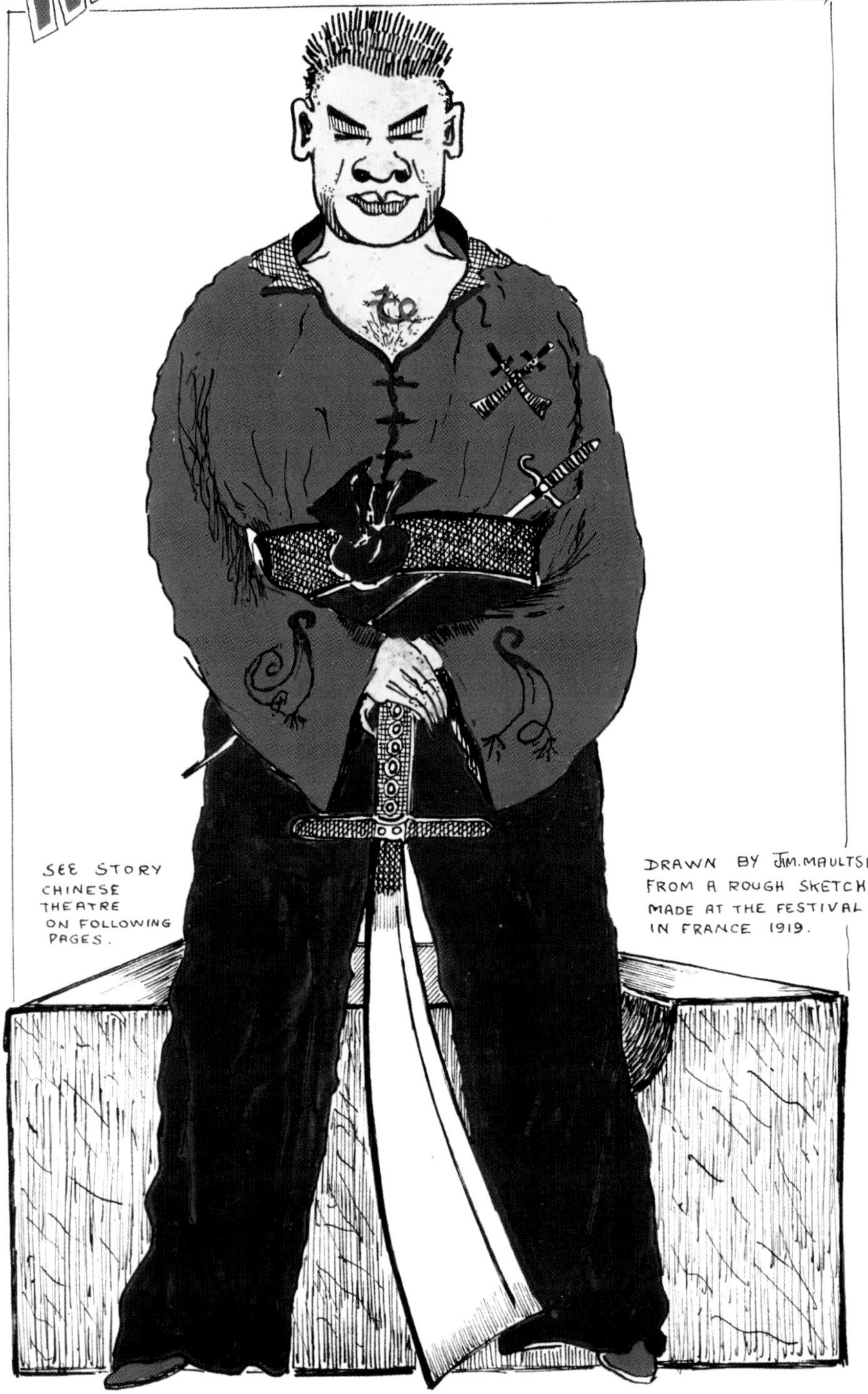

SEE STORY
CHINESE
THEATRE
ON FOLLOWING
PAGES.

DRAWN BY JIM. MAULTSAID
FROM A ROUGH SKETCH
MADE AT THE FESTIVAL
IN FRANCE 1919.

CHINESE

THEATRE

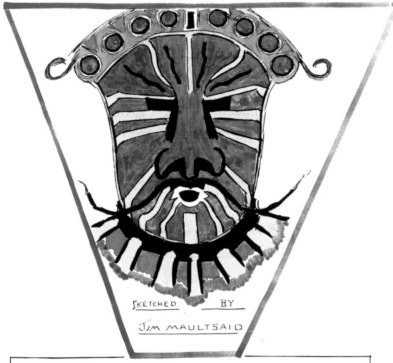

SKETCHED BY

JIM MAULTSAID

THE MOCK EXCUTATION – CHINESE DRAMA
VICTIM NO 2 STANDS BY.

1919.

CHINESE THEATRE

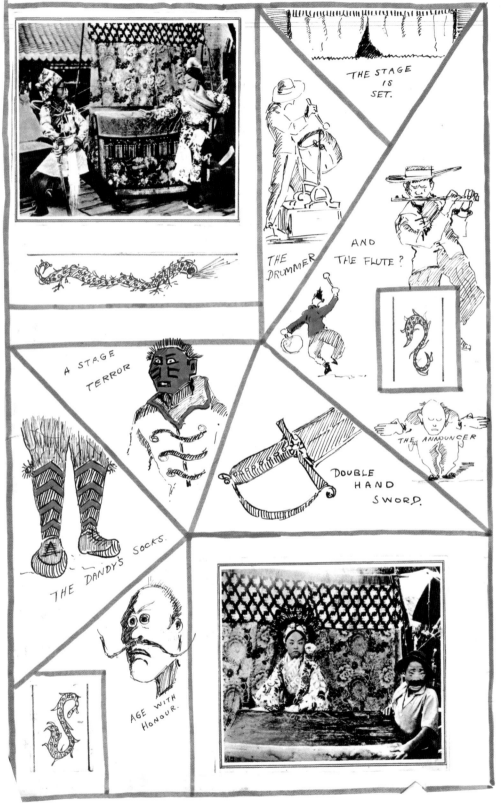

THE STAGE IS SET.

THE DRUMMER

AND THE FLUTE?

A STAGE TERROR

THE ANNOUNCER

DOUBLE HAND SWORD.

THE DANDY'S SOCKS.

AGE WITH HONOUR.

華 工 自 組 之 俱 樂 部

A SONG - A DANCE
ON A ONE STRING
— FIDDLE —

A STUDY
IN
CHINESE
MUSIC.

me – but for all that I enjoyed it thoroughly; the excitement was terrific when the 'bad man' was put in the stocks for the executioner – and I shuddered myself when his sword fell and the hideous head rolled out from the block of wood. Not his head of course, but a well manufactured one. A good trick and well carried out. Enough to give you the 'the creeps'. THE BAD MAN.

TWO DAYS ... ON – ON!

I thought this was the grand finale – but no ... on ... on ... on went that ever-lasting chatter, beating of the drums, screeching one-stringed fiddles, and other strange instruments unknown to western folk. That play lasted two whole days – and the audience, like myself, kept coming and going as we got bored, or fed up.

GOOD ACTORS

I certainly enjoyed the fun – to see some of my well-known characters in fancy dress acting a part was more than interesting, and, as usual, some of them were better actors than workers. But such is life, even in our own sphere!

A BOY - GIRL

Strange to say – all girl parts in Chinese acting is always played by a very young and active Chinese man. Ours was a 'star' in the making.

WE were greatly puzzled at the disappearance of so many five-gallon tins of methylated spirits (a valuable commodity in war days) from our barbed-wire store in the depot. Despite all our precautions – an armed sentry was even posted outside the wooden shed each day and night – yet the drums of meth walked away, on an average of one per day. What was it stolen for? How was it disposed of? And how the h★★★ was it pinched?

Three burning questions for us to get to the bottom of! Bolts and bars were of no avail. A special NCO took up duty when these drums were being loaded up – no leakage here – and our sentries were good reliable fellows, so these possibilities were all ruled out.

Weeks of this, and still the usual drum 'missing' daily. But one small point was observed now, and that was that this stealing was done during the night hours. This was something to work on. We doubled the guard – no use; more barbed wire – no use; our friends the thieves must have been enjoying the joke by now, but we were not. The old game goes on.

METHYLATED

I had a clever Sergeant called Unsworth. He came from Lancashire and he had brains. One day he reported to me that one of our platoon smelt strongly of 'meth' as if he had been drinking the stuff – and he wondered if this had any connection with the robberies?

Where did our Chinese friend get the dope?

'Very good, Sergeant! Keep it to yourself.' Sergeant Unsworth has a brainwave – and his plan was for he and I to spend a few nights down inside the old shed, just to watch and see! How's that? 'A great idea, Sergeant.' Arrangements were made with the guard to let us slip inside the shed after darkness had set in – and lock us in – then await our signal for help, or freedom.

I put it all to my commanding officer; he wished us luck on our 'wild goose chase'.

ON PATROL - FOR CHINESE

A wet, dark night. Two figures slip down the canal bank and turn towards the depot. Sergeant Unsworth and Lieutenant Maultsaid on patrol: not for Germans this time, but Chinese.

The password is given, we slide inside the wire defence and into the wooden hut. It's dark as can be, but we know our way about, and take up position. Both of us are armed, in case of trouble.

One hour ... two hours pass away. Nothing happens except the scurrying of scores of big rats – out on the prowl.

The night slowly passes and we have discovered – NOTHING! And a drum is missing! We look at each other! 'Hell!' says Unsworth, and yours truly. But wait a minute. 'Look Mister Maultsaid,' he points out the mark of a hand in the wet sand at the spot where the missing drum should have been. I jab the ground with my heavy stick, and it sounds hollow. Hot at last. Down on our hands and knees now, we claw the sand back. Wood. A wooden trap-door. Feverishly we haul it up – and a black hole, or tunnel, looms up below us. Now we have it. Here's the secret. But where does it lead to? Down goes the sergeant head first. And disappears. I wait results. Half an hour elapses. And the sergeant's voice from outside shouts to me.

Rushing out to meet him and he is covered with mud and earth, but all smiles. He has the secret!

That tunnel ran from beneath the shed right under the depot and came up outside the barbed wire some fifty or sixty yards away. What a brainwave? Now to catch them red-handed!

CAUGHT IN THE ACT

Night falls. Dark, wet and miserable. Sergeant Unsworth and I lie hidden not five yards from the mouth of the tunnel, 9.00pm. 10.00pm. 11.00pm. Still no 'stealer'. We are soaked through and through in the long dank grass. 'Hist!' The sergeant grabs my arm. A shadowy figure is up the tunnel mouth. Some scraping about, and in the figure goes. My breath comes fast, 'He's ours now, Sergeant!' We tick off the minutes awaiting his return. How time drags. Our eyes are sore straining in the darkness. We close up to the trapdoor. Here he comes; pit-a-pat goes my heartbeats. A head, shoulders, body – comes up from the earth, and out comes a drum. We spring. He offers no resistance. Scared to death, that Chinese had no fight left. Unsworth floors him and I flash a light in his face. One of my own platoon! Threats of a dire penalty and he offers to lead us to the receiving point. This is our objective. He carries the drum and we follow back to our compound. He stops at several huts. We peer through the windows, but all is quietness. At last he hesitates and, understanding his position, I give him a kick on the ★★★. He disappears. We enter the hut. Heavy breathing. Our electric lights flash. Dope! A big drum sunk into the floor ... rubber tubes ... suck away! A great capture ... see sketch on next page.

"87" NOT OUT.

A wonderful old fellow! Said he was about eighty-seven – might have been one hundred and eighty-seven. Wrinkles all over his face and a short goatee beard. Stooped down with age; beats me how the old soul ever got into France.

He had full use of all his faculties – and a sharp tongue and often, to our secret amusement, kept some of the younger fry in their places; indeed he often gave wise advice and helped us in difficult times. Truly a grand old man of China. I gave him

his place and due respect. This pleased him immensely. Said to be a bit of a prophet, the boys more or less looked upon him as the father of the flock, and so did we. Too old for hard work I gave him a job of making tea at the lunch hour for our platoon. He took a keen delight in his work and so far as I can remember never once let us down.

He had a great chum – and that chum was a sparrow! He caught it young and trained it up in his own way. A cage was built for it – more as a home of rest at night as it did not require a cage during the day.

Day and daily it went to work along with us, perched on his shoulder. Arriving on the works it was sent about its business for the morning and did not appear again until 12.00, dinner time. This finished, it flew off again and on the dot of closing time turned up once more to perch on his old hat and get carried home. Father and his bird were a 'turn'. Wonderful old fellow!

'TOMMY THOMPSON'

A thrill in every line!
It's all here.

A MAN OF MANY PARTS

ENOUGH material in this man's life to fill this book itself, but I don't intend to devote all that space to the telling of his career, so will content myself by giving you a few incidents from the pages as noted down by me in my 'war diary' 1914–19.

I had great difficulty indeed in getting the few facts that I did manage to draw from him; he was 'talkative', but not about himself. You'll understand me when I tell you that in our two years of companionship I never found out that he had a medal from the Chinese – until the day he was 'demobbed'; that comes later in the story.

A BANDIT

Early in his childhood his father and mother were murdered by Chinese bandits (still a terror in this unhappy land). They were out in the mission field spreading the word of God when their lives were cut short. 'Tommy' was spared, and taken as a prisoner away up to the mountain retreat to be brought up Chinese.

Little wonder that he could speak the language better than themselves. In fact Mr Woo said his Chinese was perfect, a great recommendation indeed from an expert. Grown-up, he soon discovered that he was not a Chinese man and his brain worked day after day perfecting his plans for escape. Out on one of the raids for plunder, his opportunity came and he took it; to me his trials and troubles of this period are as a closed book. They were terrible, I know, but he always shook his head when I tried to get details. He just said, 'Say boy! Let it slide – that part.'

RIDE HIM!

We find him away in the backwoods of Canada. Away up north as a cowboy! Out on the prairies on a wild bucking horse looking after steers. He could shoot with his big six-shooter and draw a gun like a flash! Did he not demonstrate? Not a shadow of a doubt about it – he could shoot! And he taught me the cowboy draw. Ride a horse? Yes! He said anything on four legs was easy. No horse available, the next best thing was a wild South American mule that was as yet untamed. And he got his chance.

No stirrups, no saddle – just a rope halter – and off he goes. Up and down. We scatter for safety. 'Ride him cowboy!' yells Forrester. And by heavens he rode him. He tamed that 'bucko' in half an hour. Yes, led him around like a team dog on a string. Well done, Tommy boy!

NOT FANCY TALES

Well do I remember one day he came across a Chinese swinging a heavy axe, cutting logs, and Tommy grabbed the axe in disgust to show him 'just how to use it'. The chips flew. His graceful action spoke of a proficient knowledge in the art of log cutting, proving to me that his tales of the 'back blocks' were not from fancy.

He had a spell on the footplate of the CPR as a fireman and could stoke an engine with the best, so he said, and I know he told the truth. I suppose today we could call him a 'hobo' – still he was a great wanderer and out for adventure.

TOM JOINS UP

The Great War startles the world. August 1914 sees Tom in the ranks of the gallant Canadians. Landing in France with their first expeditionary force and mixing with 'Jerry' up at Ypres, he was wounded. Sent to England, he soon gets well and again we find him in action on the Belgian front, as a motor lorry driver this time. Again disaster overtakes him and he is blown sky high on the Menin Road. Goodbye to his lorry. His days in the firing line are all over.

JUST THE MAN
The first lot of Chinese arrive in France – and Tommy is 'just the man'. On the spot, he was made a lieutenant and detailed to No. 169 Company. What joy to him! And I had the pleasure of meeting this wonderful fellow in the ranks of the Chinese Labour Corps.

MASTER LINGUIST
Fluent French came quite easily to him and he often got us out of lots of trouble. He was a master of several languages. Could lower a glass of Johnny J***** old Scotch neat, but had a heart of pure gold. His boys simply worshipped him and the work he got out of them was amazing. He taught me a lot of their customs, languages and habits. I was willing to learn and all stood me in good stead in the days to come.

RAT – TAT – TAT ... TAT-TAT
But see him in charge of the gun crew when the Hun was raiding us! The joy of battle in his eyes, he grabbed the gun himself and simply let her rip on everything, and then, on the slightest opportunity, when our searchlights got a big bomber in their grip. RAT – TAT – TAT – TAT – TAT-TAT, went Tommy's gun. Drums of ammunition simply melted away beside him.

I MISS TOMMY
The sad day arrives and we are to lose our beloved Tommy.

Demobbed sometime before me, I missed him badly indeed; and the day he left us stands out in my mind yet after all these years. It was a sad parting, and a strange one too. Let me describe it as best I can.

GOODBYE TO THE CLC
The Chinese boys got the news that he was leaving us and asked him for a few final words of fond farewell. Lined up in the compound square they silently await him.

Out strides the 'big man' and I notice he wears a medal, something I did not know he possessed. Now some of the older generation of the Chinese grasped its significance and BOWED down low – in respect. What it really meant I could not fathom, but it was for 'service' to some cause in China. A surprise to us. Time is short; he speaks to them and hopes the 'spirit' of the gods will care for them all.

I shake hands and murmur 'God be with you, Tommy boy.' I stand and watch the old order lorry slide down the French road, turn the bend at the canal bridge – and he was gone!

A GAMBLING HELL.

HOW WE RAIDED THE DEN

SURPRISED.

ONE LITTLE ROOM WAS ABSOLUTELY CAUGHT RED HANDED
THE STAKES HERE WERE HIGH — WE RAKED IN A BIG HAUL.

~ THE RAID ~

BORN gamblers, the Chinese as a rule would bet on any mortal thing. It is said of them that even two flies crawling up a wall will be the subject of a bet – on the winner. There's something in it. This is the story of how we tried to suppress their activities.

SHARKS

Now, we did not care much about what happened to the professional hardened gambler. That was his business, but we were out to protect the innocent mug from these sharks. Cards, dice, and all kinds of strange devices were employed by these gentry. We raided their huts again and again and caught red-handed a school of chance. Then a bunch were for the Officer Commanding's defaulters' parade next morning. Still it did not stop them.

BIG MONEY

It came to our ears that lots of our young boys were losing all their month's pay in a day or two at a big scale 'gambling house' somewhere in our area. But where? Big money was in the air. Big losses and big gains. All our enquiries brought no result and still the 'whisperings' went on.

An old French château standing all on its own, long since deserted, gave rise to some speculation as the headquarters of the school. Suspicion grew to certainty and we were now on the right track. Full proof came from a distracted youth who had lost all his bankbook savings, bank book and all; in fact, even his boots and clothes were pledged. Hot and reliable information this, on our promise not to give him away, or his life was not worth two 'chopsticks'. We promised.

RAIDERS

Putting all our information in front of our area commandant, we planned a raid on a large scale and with great care. We were to be fully armed as the master criminals were desperate characters and would fight like rats in a corner – so the guns were to be worn in case of resistance.

The night arrives. Darkest pitch; could not have been more suitable. We slide out in ones and twos to take up our battle positions, and all around about one hundred of us were armed to the teeth. Some strange aggressive weapons were carried – but you can read about them later. The first part of our plan was to take their outposts by storm, but quietly, so as not to alarm the main gang.

SILENCED

Creeping forward from half a dozen angles, some ten bewildered Chinese fall into our net – and never a sound. Strong hands grasped a Chinese as a big army blanket muffled his despairing cries. Then a gag was thrust into his mouth and he was trussed up.

A rap on the head finished several that struggled too much. The rifle butts rose and fell several times. The struggles ceased.

A GAMBLING HELL

ONE UNFORTUNATE ***** GOT STUCK HALF WAY THROUGH A WINDOW AND HE SUFFERED .

DRAWN IN FRANCE 1919. AFTER THE RAID.

NO ESCAPE

The way is clear for our grand finish. Outside the old house is a cordon of attackers that a fly could hardly have passed through. Into action came our light scaling ladders (built for the occasion) and up on the roof quietly scrambled the 'storm troops'. No escape that way for 'John Chinaman'. I could hear much subdued talk and cries of excitement from inside as the wheels of chance revolved. The gamblers did not dream that 'doom' was so near!

Timed to the second, all our plans had gone carefully and thoroughly as per timetable. SIZZ – sizz! A big red Very light swishes up to the sky – and throws a red glare all over the scene. Our

THE OLD FRENCH HOUSE WAS SURROUNDED. BEFORE WE ATTACKED.

signal! Battering rams, sledgehammers, rifle butts all beat a mighty earsplitting tattoo on the big massive doors. Window shutters shiver to fragments as we batter our own way in. Red flares are held aloft to shed some light on the matter.

INTO THE NET

Cries and curses from inside. All is bedlam. Cornered like rats. No escape. Yet some dashed out – and were captured. They had smashed all lamps and put lights out. We were afraid of fire.

We came prepared for this also. Hurricane hand lamps released a strange sight indeed. Tables were stacked with Franc notes of all nominations, cards scattered around, and a strange machine stood in the middle of the floor. Was it a tote? A complete outfit!

Scared Chinese men crouched in corners. Evil-faced, pigtailed, bad men scowled at us – but our six-shooters looked business-like from the muzzle end. Hands up, Johnnie!

Slowly we rounded them up, one by one. Knives were taken. So was all their cash and valuables. Not a single one escaped.

One big room was fitted up as a fruit market – oranges, apples and all the rest of Chinese fare – for sale. Very interesting was the room rigged out as a 'dope' den, and several bunks contained occupants 'out to the wide world'. Easy meat!

RED-HANDED

We took one little room red-handed. A select few here; I laughed silently as the three occupants collapsed with fright on seeing me standing at the window and a Colt revolver aimed at the one in the centre. No trouble here.

BELOVED OF FATHERS

One young boy in trying to escape through a small window had the awful misfortune to get stuck as the upper part of the sash fell on him and pinned him down with his 'parts' exposed, beloved of schoolmasters, and guarded by small boys when father is on the warpath. Poor soul his garments came undone and in the glare of the torches he was belaboured with a flat board. His screams rose above the hubbub and din.

GAMBLING KILLED

Little more needs telling. It was a great clearing out of bad characters and 'wanted men' from our district. Many were banished for good from the CLC. Some of our company were captured and, of course, had to pay the piper like the rest.

This raid had the desired effect in practically killing gambling on a large scale and at the same time landing in our net many 'much wanted men'.

DISASTER

ONE day of my life in the CLC will long be remembered by me.

Not long on French soil, our boys were green in many ways. This was only natural of course and I think if they had had a little more experience this awful experience might have been avoided.

THAT FATAL DAY

The work allotted to us this day was laying a little bogey railway track so common to the troops in war days, only in this case it was between two sets of ordinary French railway lines. We were doing very well on our job and giving satisfaction to our Royal Engineer overseers; a long line of French goods trucks was lying stationary at this particular spot as the track on other side was kept clear for through trains. This was the situation on the fatal day.

DISASTER

The light bogey rails were made up in sections, all complete for placing in position, and my squads were busily engaged in shouldering these sections from a nearby dump.

FLAMES – HORROR – DEATH...

My ears suddenly caught the sound of an oncoming train. I stop and listen. The ground trembles. The cry of warning froze on my lips. The big French engine thunders on top of us – and, horror of horrors, the leading coolies drop the rail in sheer terror.

Red flames. Grinding brakes. Death and destruction. All in the flash of a second.

How my life was spared is to me still an unsolved mystery as I was right in the midst of this awful shambles. The sight that met my horrified gaze was just a throwback to my active service days – after the smoke had cleared from the big 'Jack Johnstons' that Jerry slammed upon us when in one of his ugly moods.

DEATH! SWIFT AND TERRIBLE
CAME UPON US —

JIM. MAULTSAID

MAIMED BODIES

The end of the bogey rail when swung round had caught in the stationary trucks, and about a dozen of my platoon were swept into the inferno – red searing Hell!

Instantaneous death to some, maimed bodies to others. Utter desolation. Quickly pulling myself together, I whip off my service jacket, roll up my sleeves and commence to piece the poor shattered bits of humanity together. Poor souls, who would never again gaze on the land of their birth. Several were past all aid and the remainder dumb with shock and fright. Experience of war had taught me quickness of action and the necessity of doing something.

NEVER DIED

It is useless in describing the harrowing details of our cleaning up but in passing I may say that this disaster was the beginning of my being regarded as the 'big white man' in my platoon and this love for their officer never died until I said farewell to the CLC. It stood me in great stead in the days to come and gave me a grip on these yellow boys of mine, not by bullying methods or threats of dire punishment, but just the desire to serve their own officer.

SPARE time was always used by me for the pastime of sketching. On the opposite page you can see some of the results. All these pictures were drawn in France and cut from my sketchbook. They do look at my service in the Chinese Labour Corps. You will understand, of course, that very often conditions were all against me; paper and materials were scarce; I often worked by the light of a flickering candle stuck in the neck of a bottle and the cruel winter blasts sweeping through my place of habitation. Some of the colourings were real Chinese inks, others French. No doubt you will enjoy them as they depict a phase of the Great War not generally known to the great majority of the public: in fact I have never had the pleasure of reading a book of any kind on the Chinese Labour Corps.

CHINESE POLICEMAN.

CHINESE WHEELBARROW.

JIM.M.
1919.

NOTE THE BRASS BAND
ON WRIST WITH NUMBER
ON IT — ALSO LONG NAILS

J.M

GAMBLING DEBTS WERE OFTEN PAID
"OFF" BY WASHING CLOTHES.
WHAT WOULD OUR LOSING PUNTERS
SAY TO THIS FORM OF SETTLEMENT ?

JIM MAULTSAID.

FRANCE.
1919.

EXPERTS IN THE ART
OF SMUGGLING. WE
HAD A   BUSY TIME
SEARCHING
THEM.

JIM MAULTSAID
1919

ALL FROM
MY WAR DIARY.

C.L. CORPS.   FRANCE

No. 19462

NAME IN
CHINESE.
THUMB PRINT
RELATIVE IN
CHINA — NEXT
OF KIN

DATE .   17/10/17
AMOUNT.   50 F
COOLIE   19462
OFFICER   J. M.
COMPANY. 169
PLACE.   CALAIS

JIM.M.
'19

SAMPLE OF BANK BOOK   HELD
BY COOLIE.

With The Chinese
Labour Corps in France.

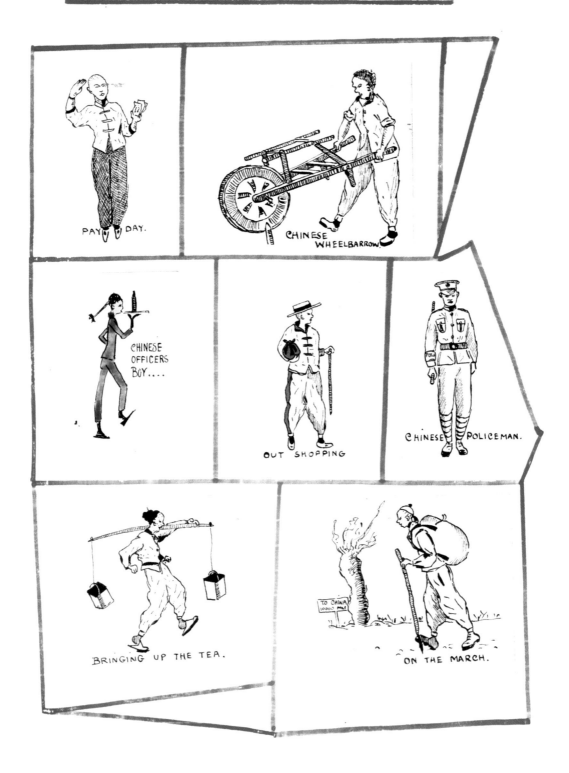

Pictures THAT ARE THE FOUNDATION—

of my stories about the C.L.C.
all drawn in France

THESE ARE THE ORIGINAL SKETCHES
AND ARE CUT FROM MY
BOOK TO INTEREST YOU I HOPE ?

JIM MAULTSAID.

A GOOD LOAD

LOADING PETROL

SHOWING YOU HIS HAIR.

DINNER HOUR

ON THE STAFF

THE photographs herewith are our bright orderly room, battalion, officers' mess, and medical department young men. Smart looking?

Of course, we picked them for these posts and trained them ourselves. Quick and adaptable as a rule, we soon had a very efficient staff that carried out our orders just as well as any white NCO or man. Note the general spick and span appearance, and pride of office attitude.

It was remarkable how quickly these lads picked up our language; being young it came to them quite easily I suppose. My own boy spent quite a lot of his time in worrying me for the meaning of 'so-and- so'. He was a cute little devil, and I had a suspicion could read me like a book, i.e. keep clear in time of trouble, and could be on the spot just at the very moment he was wanted for something in particular.

HUSH

HUSH

CONVOY'S

" HELL FOR LEATHER "

LOADING UP PETROL FOR OUR AIR FORCE.

YES! SPEAKING

THE field of operations was expanding. Our armies were operating in far-off countries. We were fighting on several battlefronts far from the Western Front. Our orders for petrol were coming in fast and furious. The cry was more, more, more. And we never failed to deliver the goods, even if it meant working twenty-four hours out of twenty-four. On the lines of supply in these days was one long 'slog', morning, noon, and night; but after all our chums up the line were going through an awful time and we would die first sooner than let them down.

UNTIL THEY COLLAPSED

We often worked our squads until they collapsed from sheer exhaustion, all for the cause.

INTO THE NIGHT

Snatching a few hours' sleep and dreaming of home, my dreams are shattered by the sound of our field telephone buzzing at a terrific rate. I scramble up, drowsily, and grab the receiver.

'Yes! Speaking.' Special rush convoy wanted for 8.00am – 'Must pull out at this hour, get me?' Headquarters speaking. Oh Lord! I'm only just in, dead beat. No help for it.

Pulling my old greatcoat on, the big heavy field boots were never off, so I was dressed.

Orders issued and a sleepy grumbling crew of Chinese follow me on the track to our petrol dump. Pitch black, the night air is damp, and the heavy guns away up there thunder out their endless challenge to the Hun. Death and destruction up there. Our boys had their backs to the wall… Oh, how well I understand. 'Come on boys! Hurry up! Sergeant Unsworth, hustle them along. Number Two Platoon – double march.' At the run we reach the dump.

FOUR THOUSAND CASES

The long line of huge French trucks stands silently awaiting arrival. Somehow they looked bigger than usual tonight. Can we ever fill them? And how in the name of the saints will we stick it? 'ZO! ZO! Come on! Here, Number Three Ganger, take these, Number Two, Number One take this.'

My orders to the platoon sergeant are rapidly given. Aircraft petrol this time, the red tins. 'How many cases, Mr Maultsaid?'

'Four thousand – and must be ready for 8.00am.' 'Can we do it, sir?' 'No "can" about it Sergeant. It must be done.' 'Very good, sir!' A fine NCO is Sergeant Unsworth.

LITTLE HEROES

Black figures scurry past. Cases crash into the trucks. No lights allowed; it's too dangerous. Bumping, swearing in Chinese, yells of pain. Slackers are kept on the stretch, we are well underway now. Little heroes work like madmen in the cold night air. Poor souls. They are weary, I know, and strained beyond endurance, almost at breaking point. Still this is war and we must do our share.

I PICTURE AGAIN

The first streaks of dawn creep into the sky; and a dull dreary-looking dawn it was. The guns still rip and roar. The ground even seems to tremble from some mighty explosion – an ammunition dump going up? My mind wanders and I picture again the boys crawling out from some filthy covering to wearily 'stand to' at the dawn. Waiting, waiting, for death. I shudder. My, it's cold; or is it that old feeling at the pit of my stomach, that somehow the troops always had at the dawn of another day?

LOADS OF DEATH

Zur! Zur! Zur! The drone of a big flight of our machines starting out for an early raid blots out all sound for a few seconds as they zoom overhead heading away towards the battle line. Big bombers loaded with death. Everything out here seems to be made to kill. Kill, kill.

STAGGER WITH WEARINESS

My eyes close for a second or two. How I could sleep, but that would never do. Crash! Crash! Crash! The boxes are being smashed into the trucks at a terrible pace. Our boys stagger with weariness across the stretch of wet sand and mud from stack to truck.

BEATING THE TIME

'Ganger! How many more to go?' 'About five hundred, officer.' I look at my watch. Good going; it's only 6.30am. We can do it easily.

'Tell the coolies, Ganger, I want a flying finish – then home. I'll see they get an extra breakfast.' He dashes away and delivers my message. I send an orderly off to camp with orders to the cookhouse sergeant (Chinese boy) to prepare double rations for No. 2 Platoon.

THE CONVOY PULLS OUT

It's 7.00am to the second – and the convoy is all complete. The last case has been hurled in, doors closed, and sealed. 'Finish a la,' yells the head Ganger. I nodded and reply, 'Ding hola. Well done boys. Quick march!'

We met our brother officers leading their platoons out for the day's work. 'A bad night, Maulty,' shouts Forrester. 'Cheerio,' pipes Thompson.

The 'Hush-Hush' convoy is now pulling out. I can hear the grunting of the engine away behind. This is the start of a long journey to ... I'm almost sure it's Italy?

'LIEUTENANT MAULTSAID will take over the command of 112 Company as from [...] in the absence of Captain [----]'

O/C COMPANY

Called away on some special errand, the officer commanding of No. 112 Company hands over his railway platoons to me. I'm now in full command of the company of rail experts. I had already had some experience of railway work as you can see by an earlier story and, truth to tell, was pleased to get this chance of commanding this outfit.

It was a chance to make good also, a change from oil and petrol dumps. The white NCOs were all expert servicemen and repair workers, so I was fairly safe from any big errors. Of course, the responsibility was all on me. Did I worry unduly? Not me! Years out here had taught me – 'what's the use of worrying?'

Only a sideline of the Great War! But now I was mixed up with railway lines – a bit harder?

JERRY SKY EYES

Tomorrow's worksheet is before me. Our job is laying track, an extension for a new depot of some kind – and as usual it had to be done at once. Away back in 1915, up at Albert, I remember a job just like this; the only difference was we had to do stuff during the night hours – in case Jerry caught us and blew us to smithereens.

Farther back this time – but still not too safe. The Huns' 'sky eyes' are always on the alert, and take a special interest in railway sidings etc., even ten, fifteen, twenty or thirty miles behind the lines.

A CLEVER SERGEANT

I detail the squads, with the help of my platoon sergeant and we make arrangements. He is a clever fellow at his work and knows exactly what is required; the only difference of opinion we had was the number of coolies he said would be required for clearing the ground and levelling out our path for the track. I cut his requirements by almost half, basing my ideas of work on what my own platoon could do, and would have to do.

BY THE MAP

Up early, the sections are ready to start. We march out in the half-light of a cold winter's morning. In due course our objective is duly reached. I called for the gangers.

In my hand I have a rough map of our work (drawn by myself the previous night) and place this on the ground, then give them a lecture, telling them how many men were to be used etc., adding that the work must be rushed at all speed. They nod approval and scurry off to their sections. I can see that I will have no slacking and my words are law. I had an idea that my own platoon had told this new lot that I was a good officer to them, also well liked, if you will pardon me saying so. I had already noted their nods of approval on parade and caught several Chinese words of satisfaction at my leadership.

'The glass is set fair.'

I blow my whistle. The day's work commences. It is not yet quite daylight.

Ground is cleared, hollows filled in, ditches and fences are flattened out. We move ahead at an amazing speed. Of course, the ground was fairly flat and no unsurmountable object was met on our route.

DOWN GOES THE RAIL

Down go the big sleepers.

Up comes the heavy rail.

Sledgehammers, crowbars, iron pegs come forward and the rail is securely nailed down. Rough work I suppose to an expert, but effective – and we are moving ahead.

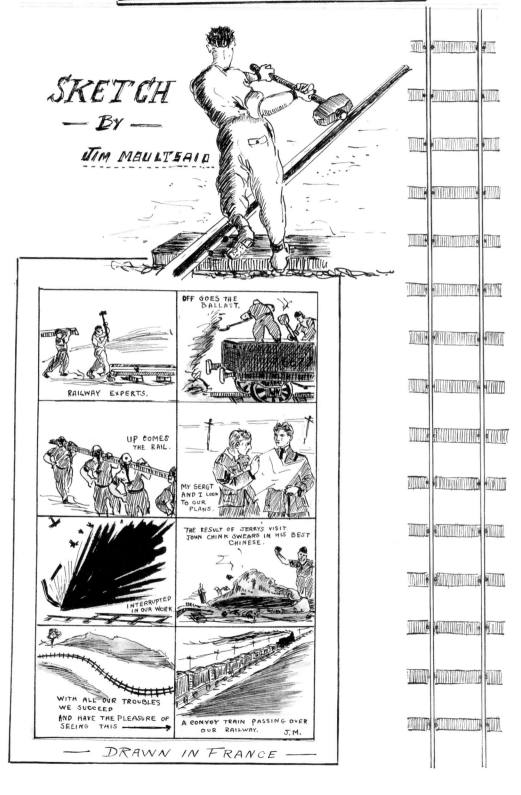

The ballast trucks are placed into position and the 'truck' gang does its work. Neat, quick, and clever, it was surprising how we crept ever onward, leaving behind us the wanted railway lines. All goes well.

FEELING PROUD

Gangs by day, gangs by night worked on the job. Day and night we hammer our way forward. As I look on the finished work, great sense of pride enters my heart – not pride in myself, but pride in my Chinese railway experts.

ONE WEEK

A week goes past. All is fair – we are well under the time limit.

UP GOES THE RAILS

Jerry raids our district. Black bombers hurl death from the skies. I do not intend describing this raid on this particular occasion – but one fine morning just after the raid we land on the 'works' to find about fifty yards of our good track in terrible disorder. Rails are twisted, sleepers like matchwood, big deep holes blown in the track. Ruined, utterly.

CHINESE CURSES

How our gangs cursed the Hun! Wonderful Chinese curse words. It was not our railway he was after, I feel sure, but unfortunately it got a big dose of bombs.

REPAIRS

Nothing for it but repair work. See sketch other side on previous page; this is cut from 'the book' and was drawn in France.

THE CONVOY PASSES

After all our troubles we had the pleasure of seeing a long convoy train pass over our track. My first job as a railway engineer was successful.

DOWN IN THE
COTTON BELT
WE WERE ENCHANTED
As he sat and sang to us.

WHEN America decided to enter the Great War she sent an advance guard across – just to learn the ropes. In this advance guard were a great many doctors. Now these gentlemen were very welcome and more so when various units of ours were strengthened by one or two of the USA boys.

My story is about a southern American doctor who came to us for experience, and he got it all right. I cannot recall his name, but it doesn't matter.

I said before 'Southern'– and I say it again – as he had no time for Tommy Thompson with his hard 'Northern' twang, yet Tommy was Canadian, not American.

A WONDERFUL VOICE

It will never leave my mind – that man's voice, soft and low. I can truthfully say I have never yet in all my travels met one like it.

I could have sat for hours and just listened. If ever a man had power in his voice, that man sure had that. A great gentleman from the South, from a world all his own.

THAT OLD BLACK MAMMIE

SLAVE DAYS

At night, when the day's work was over, he sang to us and played his banjo, wonderful artist that he was. Our Layton and Johnston of today could not have wiped his boots.

His voice? Glorious! His music? Enchanting! Sounds of the South. Songs of 'slave days' – the Cotton Belt was brought before us. To me, I could see it all in my mind's eye. And how he hated the North! His stories were full of folklore and the magic of those early babyhood and boyhood days of his. His old black nurse taught him all – and taught him well.

The old banjo twangs – he dreamily plays on, then breaks into song, 'Swanee River', 'Poor Old Joe', 'Uncle Tom' – all of them. He stops and says, 'Guess I'll tell you boys a story now?' We nod approval.

Back down the ages he goes, the trials and troubles, the sorrows of the slaves are all put on a screen for us. What a story! He wins our sympathy by the magic of his voice. We are enchanted. His old black mammie (nurse) lives again. Out one dark night, he falls over some obstacle and breaks his leg. Removed to hospital, I lose a friend. Such is life!

A SOUTHERN AMERICAN GENTLEMAN

JIM MAULTSAID

"FLASH HARRY"

"ONE of the finest stories in the BOOK!"

Sketched
By Jim. Maultsaid

'FLASH HARRY'

A BAD, BAD MAN

HE was a real bad man, this 'Flash Harry'. Where he got his nickname I cannot say. I may say that I never had the pleasure of a close up, although I came pretty near to it as you will see by the following story.

An out-and-out waster, wanted for robbery, assault and battery and several murders, you have now an idea of our friend 'FH'. He did not belong to my company, pleased to say. He was a disgrace to the CLC and a very extreme exception to the usual run of quiet, inoffensive Chinese coolies. His record was a very black one indeed. Known to thousands of workers, but his movements were shrouded in secrecy. We suspected him of spending nights in our compounds, mixing with our boys, but never got the chance to corner him. This influence must have been partial because the man that would have betrayed him would have been as good as dead. His friends would have slaughtered his betrayer; he had a few friends – from fear I suppose, not any love for him, just downright fear and, I suspect, a little fellow feeling for one of their own countrymen. They simply dare not refuse him a night's rest when the hounds of law were hot on his trail.

CLEVER? YES!

He must have been clever too, as his various disguises were known to be a French railway worker, a French soldier, a French civilian. He could speak fluent French; this was a big asset in favour of his career of crime.

WANTED ...

The authorities became so alarmed at his depredations that his photo was sent around to the various companies as 'WANTED FOR MURDER': shoot on sight – get him by any means – dead or alive.

HOW DID HE LIVE?

How did he live, you will ask? By robbery – and intimidation. He must have been sheltered by various French people at times, or he would have been stopped and questioned surely?

DETECTIVES USELESS

Chinese detectives were even brought over specially to assist in his capture but, in my opinion, they were worse than useless. They knew his past alright and that included murder I understood, but fear of the TONG or 'REVENGE' society put the breeze up these detectives. Result? NIL.

AN AWFUL DEED

His most startling deed was a fourfold murder and the victims were: an Australian soldier, a Frenchwoman and her two children, all in the one night. Horrible, savage butchery! RED ... ROARING ... HELL.

The story ran thus. He was living with a French married lady and her two little children when one night, on his return from some exploit or other, he found his lady in the arms of this Australian lover. Picture the scene! Blind animal rage. Red murder in his vile heart. A long dagger flashes. Screams of horror – and four souls pass away on their last long flight. Hell let loose this night in that home! Red ... Roaring Hell!

This was the most amazing deed.

Fleeing from the scene of carnage he became a wild haunted human, or should I say inhuman? Being devilish clever, he escaped all our nets. Satan himself must have helped him. As the story came to us we were filled with horror, and simply ached for an opportunity to get him.

WHY SHOULD HE RUN?

Coming home in the dusk along the canal bank one bleak winter's night, I was as usual at the rear of my own platoon. Somehow I sensed that my boys were uneasy, as if a strange shadow had come amongst them. What was it? I had no idea, but noticed some of them casting apprehensive glances across to the other side of the canal. I looked across. Nothing there. And yet. Yes! A figure slouched along, passed by my squads. I look, and look, drop back step by step. The figure moves quicker and quicker, breaks into a trot, then a run. I do likewise. Why should he run – and for what reason?

In my early days I fancied myself as a sprinter a little, and could still move fairly well, but that black figure gained ground. Of course, I was burdened with heavy field boots, greatcoat and six-shooter. A quarter of a mile this running contest must have covered, he on one side, and me on the other of the slow-moving canal. My wind is going, and he is gaining. Across the canal is a railway bridge. Can I reach it, and cross over?

I SHOOT ... AND MISS

The bridge at last, but my quarry is now some forty yards ahead and going like the wind. In the blackness beyond is the big railway yard. Hundreds of trucks stand there, big sheds and the hundred-and-one places of concealment. For him, safety – if he can reach it.

I pull up, six-shooter out, rest my hand on the iron parapet. Bang! Bang! Bang! Bang! Bang! And Bang! All six shots whizz after the flying fugitive. But for once my shooting powers are sadly at fault. I have missed! Missed badly. And he is gone!

To this day I am convinced in my heart of hearts it was FLASH HARRY I was shooting at.

To the best of my knowledge, he was never captured and what his ultimate end was I never found out. Perhaps even today he is one of China's leading bandits? Or he may have since died, as he had lived – a violent death?

FLASH HARRY.

CONDUCT SHEET

HIS RECORD WAS BLACK AS COULD BE

AS A FRENCH CIVILIAN

"FLASH HARRY"

THIS PICTURE IS FROM MY SKETCH BOOK AND OF COURSE IMAGINARY — BUT BASED ON HIS PHOTOGRAPH.

FEAR KEPT THE COOLIES QUIET

WANTED FOR MURDER

ASSULT AND BATTERY

RED.... ROARING..... HELL......

ONE OF HIS BEST TURN OUTS WAS IN THE — UNIFORM OF A FRENCH SOLDIER

PICTURE FROM "THE BOOK" IN FRANCE

AS A FRENCH RAILWAY WORKER

Sketches BY JIM MAULTSAID

BANG! BANG! BANG! SIX SHOTS I HAVE MISSED!

Our armies on the Western Front were being driven back, at a fast pace too, losing ground in an alarming manner. The clouds indeed were black. All our gains – on the Somme hard-earned gains – had been snatched from us in a few short months. Our line from Ypres down to the French junction was swaying. Boys and all men are flung into the gaps – the Hun is sweeping to victory. On the crest of the wave, his mighty armies press our poor tired troops back and back. Every foot of ground was paid for in flesh and blood, yet his divisions seemed endless.

The collapse of our Allies the Russians had let loose hundreds of thousands of fresh German troops from the Eastern Front. Transferred to the West, these troops were hurled against us [on 21 March 1918] as a last huge gamble to win the war. And, believe me, our folks at home never realised how near we were to complete disaster. Yet our troops fought and died in their tracks. Regiments, battalions, went into action – and never again were heard of. Lost in the welter of blood and carnage. War! War! Yes! Hellish war!

WELL DONE CLC

Why do I write this? Well, just to explain our feverish activity on the lines of communication.

We worked day and night to feed the guns, the aeroplanes, the tanks, and the troops. Wearied to death by full speed work, we were dropping off our feet almost trying to keep our end up.

Will it ever be written, the glorious part that the CLC took in this? Almost one hundred thousand of us, of the Labour Corps (Chinese section), struggled at our various tasks and when you work it out that each one of this 'hundred thousand' meant the release of the same number of British troops for the firing line you can grasp our value!

CAUGHT IN THE TOILS

Some of our CLC companies were even caught up in the toils of war, so rapid had been Jerry's advance.

THE CLOUDS DARKEN

SKETCHES BY
JIM. MAULTSAID

GLORIOUS
CHINESE LABOUR CORPS.

One story went the rounds that one of our companies (500) was captured by the enemy – and sent back to our lines with a sneering message of some kind. Numbers were killed and wounded by shellfire and bombs – yet their contract was 'Labour only' and a long way behind the lines.

Of course, these things could not be avoided as we were simply hurled back, bag and baggage, in places by the fates of war. Quite a lot of my young bloods would have even fought for us if we had been allowed – they came to me and volunteered to do so – but our job was to get the stuff up to our fighters. I often made use of my sketching ability by drawing pictures in chalk on the sides of railway trucks to explain why we had to work so hard and so long. A picture often tells a story and mine were useful. I knew the Chinese weakness for knowing what it was all about and tried to explain by sketches.

A GREAT STRAIN

Add to our worries a raid from the sky each night almost and you can dimly guess the nervous strain imposed on us even behind the lines in these dark days.

And yet I knew it was child's play compared to what our boys were getting 'up there'. At times I had a great desire and wish to be along with the old Battalion once more; and then when I looked at my arm and knew how helpless it was, well, I knew in my heart I would have been of little value as a fighting soldier and so consoled myself with the thought that I was still doing my very best to do my bit. Is it any wonder I made my platoon work so hard? I was a hard taskmaster in those days and took the last ounce out of them. I knew it was now or never with us. Our very existence depended on such units as ours.

The strain on me was appalling. I was not well myself, but prayed for strength to carry on – and did weather the storm by the help of providence and the traditional Irish qualities of 'spirit and pluck' to battle 'to the end'.

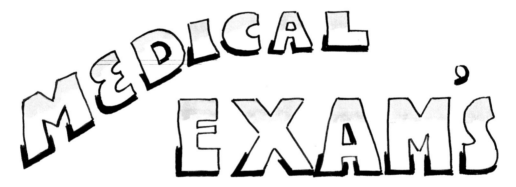

PRESSED for officers in the fighting services we had medical examinations every short period. A couple of medical officers put in an appearance and we had to appear before them for inspection.

NOT FORGOTTEN

It was only a matter of form so far as the 169 boys were concerned and I may say that not a single one of the original five ever came within a mile of being marked down as A-1; yet we knew that the doctors were told to get 'recruits' by hook or by crook. Weed us out! Half-fit even will do, yes, even quarter fit. The blank spaces must be filled, so get us the men no matter what the disability is – almost! I passed a dozen of these boards, so you will see that, although we were in the Labour Corps, we were far from being forgotten by headquarters. Boards were also held for our NCOs but again I failed to bring to mind a single man who was marked for active service.

UNFIT

After the March 1918 disaster these boards were fiercer than ever, each officer being thoroughly examined and sounded – but, as I have already told you, without result in 169 coy.

STYLE OF APPROACH

As usual it was remarkable how these medical men varied in character and style of approach. All kinds of cute dodges were tried to make us do a 'trip up' by some of them. Others were more or less casual and then an odd one had been through the mill himself and had lots of fellow feeling when he discovered your weakness was from wounds received in battle. A weak spot for one of the boys – and all our boys had already fought a good fight on some front or other – so we were more or less privileged to some small extent. These exams for all that had an unsettling influence on us for some days after; yet they had to be endured.

One fine evening, as I was returning from a day's weary toil at the rear of my platoon, a motor lorry pulled up beside me and I was hailed by an officer, his rank being a major so far as I could see. He stood up and addressed me as follows, 'Jump in here at once young man.'

I was surprised to get such an order and, coming closer to the lorry, it struck me as peculiar that it was packed already with officers, mostly second lieutenants like myself.

What the h★★★ did he want me for? This was the thought that flashed through my brain. Full of pomp, that major fellow gave me an instantaneous dislike to him; why I don't know but I put him down as our 'bluffer', and he was a rookie. Never heard a shot fired in anger I knew. 'Why should I get into the lorry?' I parried!

'We want all spare officers up in the line at once,' he replied.

'Oh!' I said, 'I don't think I'm what you would call a "spare" officer.'

JUMP IN!
'Look here young man – jump in!' He was getting angry now. Interested faces peered down at me. 'Where is your authority to order me like this,' was my next question? My hundred odd Chinese men were now gathered around me – they had missed me, turned back and stood dumbly at my side, not knowing the meaning of the 'palaver'.

'My advice to you is – jump in,' he barks now. I do not obey. Taking my officer's book from my breast pocket I reach him my certificate of service and medical report 'unfit for service B2'. 'When I'm fit for the line again the Medical Officer will certify me to this effect,' I said. 'We have an exam each week. I refuse to get into the lorry without my commanding officer's authority. Show me that and I'll go at once.'

I knew he could not do so and, 'Furthermore, what is to happen to these Chinese boys of mine?' By a strange irony of fate I have not a single NCO with me on this particular evening. Waxing hot, I added that I have already fought the good fight 'up there' and suffered too – in fact was still suffering. 'Yet you want me to go back?' 'Yes!'

I know men are wanted badly – but there are hundreds of thousands who have not yet tasted 'fire' – let them have a chance first. 'No Sir! I do not board your lorry. Good afternoon!'

He gasped! Swallowed hard, and was beaten. 'Drive on,' he ordered. I salute and step back, into the gloom.

MY FATE?

Gathering my amazed Chinese men once more, I order them to form up and 'ky-by-zo' (quick march).

I often wondered what my fate would have been if I had deserted my platoon on that fateful day.

STARTLED one fine morning by a very urgent call – 'Come quick. Come see' – I hurried after my boy, and he led me to our compound huts. Early as it was in the morning, all the coolies seemed to be up and about and excitement was at fever pitch. Jabbering like a pack of monkeys, I did not follow what all the 'bother' was as they trotted after me – but I was soon to get a shock.

EARLY MORN.....
SMASHING BLOWS
.....MURDER.......

WHAT A SIGHT!

What a sight met my gaze! Blood and brains scattered against the side of the sleeping bunk – a ghastly huddled form, arms thrown wide, head and face battered to pulp. Ah, it was – sickening! Hardened as I was to all forms of death and destruction, I shuddered at the sight of this brown body with horrible head. Clearly a case of murder. Indeed the weapon of destruction lay across the victim's legs: a big railway sledgehammer, all covered with red, red blood and hair.

No Sexton Blake or Sherlock Holmes required to assist you in coming to this conclusion. Murder! Pure and simple murder!

This was in the Railway Company, and not my own, but quick steps would have to be taken to get the murderer. He could not yet have travelled far if he was 'on the run'.

Flash Harry! Is it his work?

I dismiss the thought at once for some reason – it did not look like his style. Rarely did he murder his own sort. The sergeant major was ordered to get through to HQ and our military police at all speed on the field telephone. All 112 Company are confined to camp.

Events move swiftly.

The hut was cleared – not a thing around the body was in any way disturbed. Sentries were posted to keep the curious coolies back from the spot.

HQ MOVE SOME

Our headquarters moved at great speed and in a remarkable short time had detectives, interpreters and Red Cross squads up in a motor lorry to take over the case.

THE THIRD DEGREE

Every man was questioned very minutely and carefully, one by one. How that morning dragged! You will be disappointed no doubt when I tell you that there was no brilliant detective work necessary in finding the murderer. Several coolies were taken aside for a third-degree examination, sifting the wheat from the chaff. One was suspected, a mild inoffensive looking youth. Scared to death, I thought, and yet he did not look the part.

HE WAS THE MAN ...

Handcuffs are clamped on him. He is hustled to the guardroom. Special guards are posted.

We feel we have got the right man. Our Mr Woo tells me it looks bad against him, and under his breath whispers 'revenge' – a case of 'he was the man detailed for the execution' and had to do his work, or he would have been the victim himself. Mr Woo's summing up, 'but for the love of all the forefathers Mr Maultsaid, keep this to yourself!'

GUILTY MINDS

All the evidence is gathered bit by bit. We resume our railway construction work next day as usual, but a dark pall of evil somehow hangs over our squads. Small groups discuss the murder, and the plotters tremble in their shoes, I suppose? Would the prisoner squeal? Knowing that for him there was nothing but the firing squad.

HIS MISFORTUNE

In due course the trial took place. The prisoner admitted that he had no ill will against the dead man – but his misfortune was indeed great when he drew –

'THE DICE OF DEATH'

The murdered man had in some way incurred the displeasure of his secret society. You can picture that fatal committee meeting … planning his death … and the cunning method employed of drawing lots to pick the gunman, or 'executioner'!

Just like Chinese methods.

WOULD NOT SPLIT

Did the prisoner confess? No! He did not. And all the pressure brought to bear on him to sell his comrades was of no avail.

DEATH …

No shadow of doubt remained in the minds of the court martial judges. We had the right man. And the dreaded sentence of death was passed.

A STRANGE REQUEST

A cold winter's morning. A little party slowly wends its way across the sand dunes. A stake is driven into the ground and the blindfolded shrinking coolie tied to it. He speaks in Chinese. His request is a strange one. Take the bandage off his eyes, and let him die like a British soldier. Marvellous!

GRANTED

His request is granted.

THE END …

A sharp order. A volley rings out, echoes and re-echoes away down the sand dunes. His head drops forward. Poor soul, the spirit has gone, gone to meet …

THE LAST LINE

'Weary limbs, but stout hearts, still beat beneath that khaki jacket.'

ORDERS came through to the area commandant that all white NCOs and men belonging to the labour battalions in categories ABC and B1, B2 and B3 were to be taken in hand at once in regard to some training in the use of firearms etc. In plain words, 'efforts were to be made at once to make these cripples into some kind of fighting soldiers.'

When you think of it, 99 per cent of these men had bad legs, bad arms, bad sight, bad chests, bad everything. Not an A1 man in one thousand, you have some idea of the formidable work before the area CO. Hundreds had never fired a rifle – in fact did not know one end from the other. The majority could not even 'form fours'.

OVERTIME

This work was to be undertaken after the ordinary day's work was over. Ye Gods! Our day's work was from dawn till dusk!

NOT US

The order did not affect our company as every man-jack had been through the mill – all were wounded on the field of battle – so we did not worry. Of course, we carried out our orders and gave a few lectures etc. to brighten up their rusty knowledge in the art of being a 'real soldier' once more.

CAREY'S ARMY

Real business was enacted in the white labour battalions. 'Drilling', 'shooting', 'care of arms', all the usual, as best they could and it was poor material to work on. Poor fellows – not a sound man amongst them, yet they tried to do their best. Did not the Labour Corps fight in the defence of Albert – and get great praise from Sir Douglas himself? They did! And fought a good fight too! General Carey's Army!

The whole idea was, if things came to the worst (remember please that the Germans were sweeping onwards nearer and nearer to the all-important Channel ports), that these Labour Corps boys would be thrown into the gap. Our badge was the Pick, Shovel and Rifle. A fine combination – what say you?

Of course I had many smiles to myself when I looked at some of their antics. I could see the look of horror and disgust on Regimental Sergeant Major Alfick's face (of 14 RIR (YCV)) as he bellowed 'Fred Karno's Army' at us in our rookie days. What he would have called this outfit, only a sergeant major could tell you!!

IF JERRY

For all that, it was wonderful how they progressed – these crippled boys and old men.

Quite an interest taken in all their drills and lectures. Willing to learn and do their best. For we all knew in our hearts that things were bad, black indeed, and not a shadow of doubt about it – it would be a case of fight or into the sea you go, all of us. Yes, right in, no escape, if Jerry broke through our front.

THE PICK SHOVEL & RIFLE

DID NOT THE LABOUR CORPS FIGHT IN THE LAST DITCH AT ALBEIT?

THEY DID!

FROM SIR DOUGLAS HAIGS REPORT

JIM. MAULISAT

Carey's Force.

(37) The whole of the troops holding the British line south of the Somme were now greatly exhausted, and the absence of reserves behind them gave ground for considerable anxiety. As the result of a conference held by the Fifth Army Commander on the 25th March, a mixed force, including details, stragglers, schools personnel, tunnelling companies, Army troops companies, field survey companies, and Canadian and American engineers, had been got together and organised by General Grant, the Chief Engineer to the Fifth Army. On the 26th March these were posted by General Grant, in accordance with orders given by the Fifth Army Commander on the line of the old Amiens defences between Mézières, Marcelcave and Hamel. Subsequently, as General Grant could ill be spared from his proper duties, he was directed to hand over command of his force to General Carey.

Except for General Carey's force there were no reinforcements of any kind behind the divisions which had been fighting for the most part continuously since the opening of the battle. In consideration of this fact and the thinness of our fighting line, the Fifth Army Commander did not deem it practicable for our troops to attempt to maintain the Hattencourt-Frise positions if seriously attacked. Accordingly, orders had been given on the night of the 25th March that, in the event of the enemy continuing his assaults in strength, divisions should fall back, fighting rearguard actions, to the approximate line Le Quesnoy-Rosières-Proyart. This line was intended to link up with the right of the Third Army at Bray.

No wonder we were serious minded! And the old flame still lived in the breasts of warriors of Mons, Ypres, Hooge, Hill 60, Loos, the Somme – the fighting spirit beloved of battalion commanders. We could fight again, shoulder to shoulder, if pressed into the service of Sir Douglas, and would not let him down. How our great chief was loved by his men. A great leader of men, God-fearing and true. One of the greatest of the Great War, who never got a fraction of the praise or honour he was so justly entitled to.

BY JIM MAULTSAID.

NIGHT after night they came after us!

The months of March and April 1918, during the great German push for the grand breakthrough on the Western Front, were marked by hectic activity on his part in the air. Back areas were bombed by day and by night, especially the night hours of darkness. Causing desolation of supplies and hindering our supply services. And, of course, we got our share. Practically every night for weeks on end it was 'air raid', 'air raid'; we were worn to a shadow by duties all day with our squads of Chinese, and night duties at our posts in the machine-gun emplacements.

SURROUNDED BY DEATH.

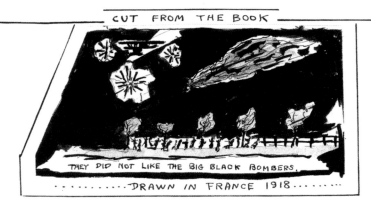

CUT FROM THE BOOK

THEY DID NOT LIKE THE BIG BLACK BOMBERS.

· · · · · · · · · · DRAWN IN FRANCE 1918 · · · · · · · · · ·

SURROUNDED BY DEATH

Surrounded as we were by dumps of petrol, oil, spirit, motor-lorry spare parts, hay and clothing, it was like dropping a match in a tin of paraffin oil to have the misfortune of a big bomb in our midst.

FLEEING IN TERROR

Our system of foghorn signals gave us a chance to be on the alert when the 'Skyhawks' were coming. How the Chinese boys hopped to it when the first blast split the air! Every man-jack of them got up, grabbed a blanket and away out the old French roads as fast as their legs would carry them. This was really a good thing for us in a way as it took them off our hands for the moment. No such escape for the white officers and NCOs; we had to 'stand to' at our air stations: field guns, anti-aircraft guns, machine guns and Lewis guns.

WHAT A SHOCK

'THE DUD'

S-w-i-s-h ! We duck. It's a dud! Let me tell you the story of that supposed 'dud' bomb.

Straight down it came, missed a sentry of ours by a foot or two, slashed into the soft earth, then exploded – and the blowback blew his rifle to bits, his tin hat, his overcoat and burned his tunic; yet not a scratch on the man himself. What a shock! And that self-same bomb just missed the buried petrol pipe line by a foot or so. I shudder at the thought of 'what might have been'.

INSTRUMENTS OF HELL

Crash! Bang! Crash! Zipp – Zipp. Flames shoot up. We gasp, choke and curse. Eight or nine mighty explosions rend the air. We are thrown in a heap as these aerial torpedoes hurl themselves through space to burst with a roar like a thousand claps of thunder, bringing the blood to our noses and ears, infernal instruments of hell itself. Dropped from the sky thousands of feet up, well out of range.

Next day we find the big craters all in a straight line right in the centre of the petrol dump.

Heavens above! And we all escaped!

RED INFERNO

THE sky lights up – stays lit.

Red flames away behind us.

By G★★ he has got something tonight! The red glow mounts to the very heavens, or so we think, and does not die down.

What is it?

The news next morning was staggering. A big motor-tyre depot had got it fair and square and caught fire: a direct hit. The blaze was terrific and the heat overpowering. A general of ours took command of a party of men and rushed out from the bombproof dug-outs to try and save the depot. That Black Hawk has the nerve to sweep down and open fire on the salvage squad. Round and round he circles, like an evil bat of prey. His work that night was stupendous from the German point of view as he killed many, including the general.

CUT IN HALF

I remember a French dwelling house cut clean in two, like a loaf cut in two halves. There stood the one half – open to view, beds in their position, tables as usual, and the pictures on the walls – and the other half, blown to fragments.

A most unusual sight. I cannot remember what happened to the family but I think some were 'taken' and some were 'left' to curse the Germans until their lives' end. And no wonder!

BELIEVE IT OR NOT

PoW camps were scattered around; compounds of German troops captured by us. A story that went the rounds was this: after a fierce raid one night in which a certain Chinese camp suffered some awful experience and lost a few of their best chums, the German camp was broken into and in the morning around a dozen or so of the Huns were found with their throats neatly slit. Chinese revenge? Eastern methods? True or untrue, I cannot vouch for the story, but personally I believed it – and why not?

WEEKS OF IT

Terror from the sky! Weeks of it.

ZUR! ZUR! ZUR!

THIS was how the German air force supported their armies on the ground.

DROVES OF THEM

Night after night. Relays of them. Droves of them zooming through the black sky. Zurr! zurr! zurr! We could pick a Hun out miles away.

Don't imagine they got it all their own way, not by a long chalk. Our boys went up and met them, and gave battle. Our guns thundered out, ripping the air with thousands of shells – yet as a rule they seemed to bear charmed lives, those German airmen.

VAIN EFFORTS

C – R – A – S – H! Here they come again. Bang! Swish – swish! Whizz!

No warning this time. We rush for our tin hats, sound the gong and scamper away for 'Fire posts'. What a h★★★ of a life!

Rat-tat-tat-tat. Belts of bullets slide through our machine guns, tracer bullets stabbing the sky. Searchlights cross, sweep around in the effort to pick him up. We shiver – and sweat – and curse those b★★★dy 'black bombers'.

BACK TO MY OLD LOVE

My days as the officer commanding No. 112 were over. I had handed the 'skipper' his squads back again and I received my 'all clear' papers duly signed and sealed by him. My work as a railway expert was ended.

Glad to get back to my old love, my platoon were delighted to have their very own officer back once more. The Chinese are funny that way. Once they settled down to a particular man in charge, they simply hate changes. Therefore great joy indeed at the return of 'yours truly'.

My term with the railmen had been quite happy, but tragic too, as you have already read. However, life in these days was swift, little time to sit and mope. Change, partings, death even, came somehow more or less as a matter of course.

It was ever 'move onward', live today, for tomorrow may never come; and for many it never did.

Such were the years 1914–1918.

THE END

JIM. MAULSAID -   from an original DRAWING - exact copy.